Fortune Cookies Of Real Estate

Turning 70,000 to Millions

by

Sal Kapunan, Ph.D., Ed.D.

Images by the Author

Bloomington, IN  Milton Keynes, UK

AuthorHouse™
1663 Liberty Drive, Suite 200
Bloomington, IN 47403
www.authorhouse.com
Phone: 1-800-839-8640

AuthorHouse™ UK Ltd.
500 Avebury Boulevard
Central Milton Keynes, MK9 2BE
www.authorhouse.co.uk
Phone: 08001974150

First published by AuthorHouse 9/27/2006

ISBN: 1-4259-5044-2 (sc)

Printed in the United States of America
Bloomington, Indiana

This book is printed on acid-free paper.

Sal Kapunan has written the following books:

1. My Taoist Vision of Art (Parkway Publishers, 1999)
2. Surviving WWII As A Child Swamp Hermit (1st Books Library, 2002)
3. Everyone Is An Artist: Making Yourself The Artwork (IUniverse, 2003)
4. The Child Daredevil Hero (AuthorHouse, 2004)
5. Fortune Cookies of Real Estate Investing, Illustrated by the author (Author House, 2006)

Dedication

I dedicate this work to my brother-in-law, Murray Zucker, and his wife, Elaine. He graduated from the famous Wharton School of Business in Philadelphia and was my model and mentor for making creative and effective business decisions.

I became computer literate because of his suggestion to buy a personal computer in 1981 especially for keeping financial records. Even though I have not yet used the Spread Sheet software, as he had encouraged me to do, I have discovered the Word Processor, which has made writing much easier and a great pleasure!

He and Elaine have encouraged and supported all my endeavors especially in writing books on various topics.

Acknowledgments

I thank my wife, my wonderful friend and companion for allowing me to resume my writing again. I stopped writing for six months after she complained that she felt like a widow when I spent too much time on the word processor. I'm sorry, sweetheart, for doing that to you. I promise to cut back on the time I spend typing.

I also thank my family and relatives in the Philippines and in America for their encouragement and support.

I thank the High Country Writers for bestowing awards on my books during the last three years. I have been able to say truthfully, "I'm an award winning author."

I will not allow these awards to change me in any way, except to feel more grateful for all the help I have received from the members during the last five years. I do appreciate these public recognitions of my efforts.

You're all wonderful colleagues and friends!

Table of Contents

Introduction

An Ode to Leveraged Real Estate Investments

Investing, per se, is a necessity!
You need to increase the value of your savings.
You need your money to work for you
 'cause you don't know how long you'll live.
You might not be able to afford your retirement.

But investing is risky and you can lose all your money!
That's why you must minimize your investment risks.
You must diversify by investing in different instruments.
Don't put all your eggs in one basket.
You could drop the basket and break all the eggs.
Don't invest in commodities.
You're, in fact, investing in futures.
If you don't know the future, you may not have any future.

Be careful when investing in stocks.
They go up or down for no valid reason.
Today, they go down because the brokers are taking profits.
Tomorrow, they go up for the same reasons.

And, why bother with mutual funds?
They are also made up of stocks and bonds.
Like stocks, they also go up or down.
They go up and down while managers are making profits.
Retail business is hard and risky.
If you're not well capitalized, you'll go bankrupt in a jiffy.
And, wholesale business is even harder and riskier.
When you go bankrupt, you may lose all your money!

The best investment I know of is leveraged real estate.
It gives you more control of your money and inventory.
You can buy properties by using other people's money.
You can even buy properties with no money down.
Once an investment property has been established,
It keeps on growing on its own.
Your investment grows through cash flow, equity growth,
Tax shelters and open market demand.
If the demand exceeds supply, the property naturally appreciates.
Your total return may exceed 200%, which is awesome!
In boom markets, an investor may rake in 2000% or more!

Invest in real estate and be a self-made millionaire!
You'll sleep more soundly and dream creative dreams.
You'll be less stressed out and maintain your youth.
Your best reward is a long happy life that you can afford.
This is heaven on earth and you shouldn't ask for more!

****

This short free verse poem was purposely written, in February 2006, to serve as an appropriate introduction for this book.

The reader should also note that this book is not a work of fiction. It belongs to the category of "creative non-fiction." What it means is that the author has taken the liberty to change some names for the sake of privacy and to disguise the identity of some characters so as to save them from identity theft. Identity theft is the largest crime wave that has plagued the country. It is threatening to destroy our credit system, which is essential to modern progress!

Both Yeta and Pol had been identity theft victims! Hence, the "creative non-fiction" device was intended to obfuscate the truth as much as possible! In other words, the declarative sentences in the book shouldn't be taken literally! The author suggests to try reading between the lines!

The creative non-fiction part of the book consists primarily in narrating in the third person! This devise allowed the author greater freedom to use dialogues and to introduce more characters when he deemed it necessary.

However, this is not a "how to" book that spells out the minute details of real estate investing and transactions. More accurately, this is a true story of a couple of middle-aged professionals who had been disenfranchised from their careers because they were too old or because their specialties had been deemed old fashioned and impractical! Forced to find a different livelihood from what they had trained to do, they quickly taught themselves the rudiments of real estate investing and created their own jobs by going into a leveraged real estate investment business.

This is an unbelievable story of how a virtually penniless couple, who had just gotten married, made a lot of money by investing in a financial instrument they knew little about! They succeeded and survived financially because they had to! Hence, this is essentially a success story of *survival in America*! This is an American success story!

Using $70,000 as their start up capital, they turned this small amount of money into millions of dollars in just four years! They did so well financially that in just five years in leveraged real estate investing, they retired to Florida on July 25, 1985!

They liquidated their properties in Philadelphia and invested in the stock market. They were both flying very high as they rode a bull market! Then, suddenly, in 1987, the stock market collapsed and they lost half of their assets! They liquidated all their stocks and mutual funds and returned to leveraged real estate investing. They hired two builders to construct single family rental houses starting in 1988.

By 2004, they had recouped all their losses and moved ahead financially because they followed the same sound formula that made them successful in 1980! Now, there is no looking back!

Chapter One.
Coming To America

Salvador Kapunan, Jr. obtained his doctorate in philosophy from the prestigious Pontifical Santo Tomas University in Manila in 1960. He accepted his first teaching job at Notre Dame University of Cotabato City. He taught various subjects in philosophy for five years.

Doctoral Graduation Photo

After only five years of teaching, he felt burnt out because every day he made seven class preparations and had no leisure time. He shared his frustrations with other professors who had been born and raised in the United States. They told him that, as far as they knew, professors in America taught no more than four courses a day. In fact, they also told him that senior tenured professors taught only two or three seminars, assisted by a couple of graduate students. He wished his teaching load were only four courses!

Moreover, he had other serious differences of opinion regarding educational policies with the administration and felt he had to resign.

He had gotten into raucous arguments with the president of the college over what Sal thought was an antiquated system of grading! He was <u>advocating a pass-fail system of grading</u>!

For these reasons, he wanted to immigrate to America, where he expected to be more free and prosperous. He already knew that if he chose to teach in the USA, his teaching load would be much less!

****

As revealed in his memoirs, *Surviving WWII as a Child Swamp Hermit* (1stbooks Library, 2001), Sal found himself illiterate when he took a short third grade refresher course in 1946. His teacher knew he was <u>illiterate</u>; yet, instead of sending him back to first grade where he could learn the alphabet all over again, the teacher promoted him to fourth grade after five months of learning virtually nothing. After another five months, the school promoted him again to fifth grade and he was still illiterate!

It was in fifth grade when his whole academic life completely fell apart! For the first time, all his classes were held in a building with a roof over their heads in downtown Mambusao.

During the past two years, his classes were held under large trees where they got wet every time it rained. They had no pencils or paper. They used banana leaves to write on by using sharpened sticks as pencils. What the sharpened stick did was to drain the water from the banana leaves. Those who could read and write could see what had been scratched on the surface for about ten minutes. After that time, the banana leaf shriveled up and it was difficult to discern what had been written. He was going to "school" in a backward barrio that was completely deprived of school supplies!

In fifth grade, he had text books for each subject. Being still illiterate, however, he couldn't even read the titles of the books. But, his new and bigger shock was in finding out suddenly that the new medium of all instructions was a foreign language called English, which was completely foreign to him. In Barrio Libo-o, while in his fourth grade class, the medium of instruction was a vernacular called Illonggo. The vernacular was not even used as a transitional medium. The teachers took it for granted that all the pupils knew English.

Predictably, <u>he failed every subject at every grading</u> period! He was hoping the school would expel him or send him back to first grade where he could learn literacy! He had no such luck! All the <u>teachers simply ignored his illiteracy!</u>

Sal expected to receive failing grades like 50 or 60. Instead, the teachers gave him the grade of 75 on every subject, which, on paper, was a passing mark. Giving him passing marks was both a lie and a cruel act! The grade of 75 placed him in an <u>academic limbo</u> which kept him in school and couldn't drop out. The amazing thing about the fiction of having passing grades of 75 was that he may eventually <u>graduate as an illiterate</u>! Such graduates were later on called "functional illiterates," which really meant that they couldn't function at all in a civilized society. They lived and functioned as if they had never gone to school!

Sal could not accept being in a false academic bubble! Internally, he was wilting away and dying in shame and utter embarrassment! The members of the Kapunan clan had a good professional, social and political reputation and Sal felt that he was dragging his family in shame! To save the family from an on-going embarrassment, he felt that it was better for him to disappear somehow! He could run away and change his name. However, he knew that such an alternative was almost impossible to sustain since he had no survival skills especially in a chaotic post war economy!

He considered going back and resume his hermitic life in the swamps; however, he was too depressed to think that such a life was worth living!

He thought that the logical thing to do was to take his life by <u>drowning</u>! He figured out that if he tied a rope to a tree and placed a lasso around his neck, the velocity of the river current would suffocate him to death! He hoped that a crocodile might take care of his body before his family found out what had really happened!

At around ten one evening, when everyone was already asleep, he walked to the bank of the river, which was only a block away. He was perfectly calm and believed in the rightness of his decision! After making the necessary rope attachments, he closed his eyes and said 'goodbye' to his beloved Philippines, his province of Capiz and town of Mambusao, to his parents, brothers and sisters and every relative he could remember. After he felt ready, he simply jumped into the water and waited to feel the pain around his neck! He expected to loose consciousness within five or ten minutes!

He did feel the pain but, even after what seemed like twenty minutes, he was still conscious. Obviously, the water velocity was not strong enough to strangle him. All of a sudden, he felt chilly and decided to remove the noose around his neck and decided to return home. Home was with Captain and Mrs. Juan Mansilla. Catalina, Juan's wife, was Salvador senior's first cousin. Junior intended to try again when the water level in the river was higher.

He went to sleep very soundly and that night, he had an unexpected <u>didactic dream</u>! In his dream, he was playing with wooden blocks that contained the letters of the English alphabet. In the beginning, he was just randomly picking up the blocks and played with them in various ways. Then, he combined the blocks so that they formed syllables. Then, he added more syllables so that he formed words. Then, out of the words, he formed sentences and the sentences became paragraphs. The paragraphs became stories!

When he woke up, he clearly understood the meaning of the dream! His <u>subconscious mind</u> was telling him that he was wrong in assuming that only teachers taught pupils how to be literate. His mind was telling him that <u>he could learn how to read and write on his own</u>. Having teachers would help but they were not absolutely necessary. All he had to do was, like in the dream, to combine letters, syllables, words, paragraphs and weave them into marvelous stories! The stories could be anything. They didn't have to be true, like in fiction. He also realized that, with the aid of a big dictionary, he could also teach himself English and many other languages.

These new insights solved the inherent problems! Those new possibilities gave him hope that, in time, he would be literate and, therefore, precluded taking his life! However, he knew that it would take him years to become literate in English, Tagalog and Illonggo.

In order to save his family from shame and embarrassment, he must completely apply himself every day to become literate; and he must radically change his class ranking from the bottom to the top!

He worked as hard as he knew how! After the first year of learning to read and write, on his own, the whole endeavor seemed hopeless! His grades were still all 75s, which everybody knew were really failing marks! Still, the grades didn't really matter because he knew that every day he was improving! It was just a question of time! He couldn't be sure when his literacy efforts would change his grades.

When he was promoted to sixth grade, he knew that at the end of that year, he would graduate from the elementary school. (Even though the Philippine school system was modeled after the US system, the Philippine schooling differed from its model by eliminating the middle grades. From the elementary school, students went right into high school and from high school right into college).

The thought of graduating from the elementary school with some passing marks drove Sal even harder! His goal was very modest. He wanted to move his grades up from 75 to 78 or 80. Still, if he saw an 80 mark on his grading card, that slight movement would have proven <u>success</u> for his solitary endeavor!

When he graduated from the elementary school in June 1949, his average grade was 78. The highest grade he received was 82 in English!

He enrolled in high school at the new Mambusao High in town. He foresaw that his grades would improve as his literacy improved. Still, his grades were just mediocre.

After he finished his inconspicuous second year in high school, his parents moved the entire family to Cotabato in Mindanao, which was a Muslim land. The large island of Mindanao was inhabited by Muslims, whom the Spaniards and Filipinos called *Moros*. The Moors of Africa had conquered and occupied southern Spain for centuries. Hence, the term Moros was tinged with anger and derision!

The Philippine Commonwealth obtained its <u>independence from America in July 1946</u>. Shortly after its independence, the Philippine legislature made <u>Tagalog</u>, the dialect spoken in Manila and its environs, as the <u>national language</u>.

The Philippine government also passed <u>a homestead law</u> which awarded 24 hectares of land to every male Christian who was 18 years or older. The law entitled his father and his three older brothers to so much land in the Koronadal Valley in a new town called Norala.

The Homestead Act was part of the necessary conditions for giving the Philippines its independence from the United States. The Homestead Act would force the integration of Christians and the Muslim in Mindanao.

The US governor of the Philippines was able to acquire large tracts of lands that belonged to Muslim Chiefs, locally known as Datus. The Datus agreed to cede the lands for large sums of money and the "political carrot" of governorship of their respective Provinces.

The Muslim governors could maintain their political positions indefinitely, as long as they were re-elected by their constituencies. Since the Muslims were predictably in the majority, the Muslim governors would govern *ad infinitum*.

Unfortunately, the Christian migration to Mindanao continued long after all the available lands had already been given away! As a result, the Datus couldn't hold on to power because by 1952, the majority of the voters in Mindanao were Christians! The Christian migration to Mindanao was .like an avalance!

****

The Kapunan family arrived in Norala in July 1948. There was a brand new three-bedroom house waiting for the large family of ten children (7 boys and 3 girls). The house was situated on a small stream, filled with tilapia, cat fish and many other types of fish. The house was close to the center of the town of Norala. The town was relatively small, with only about 2000 residents.

The rest of the population was scattered in the surrounding villages called *Barrios*. The homestead farms were scattered in various barrios. The Kapunan farms, which was almost 100 hectares, were situated in Barrio Cinco (Fifth Barrio).

Not long after their arrival, Salvador, Senior became a close friend of Datu Kudanding, the new governor of Cotabato province. Badong, as his friends called him, was able to negotiate the purchase of another 100 hectares of land from the governor in the town of Kolambug.

All the older and younger boys were immediately sent to the farms to start cutting down the grass, which were mostly *cogon*.

After cutting down all the grasses, then they built rice paddies, which divided the fields into rectangular sections.

The paddies were earthen embankments, designed to trap and corral rain water. As soon as rain water had filled the paddies, plowing the fields could then begin.

Plowing the fields softened the soil and the water killed the weeds and the grasses. Within weeks after the paddies had been filled with water, different kinds of fresh water fish were swimming around. Catching fish became an interesting past time!

Even though Sal had been born in a farm in Barrio Libo-o, he had never worked as a farmer or a farmer's helper. He quickly found out how hard farm work was! The tropical heat and humidity just sapped the worker's energy! It was necessary to rest and drink water often or they would get dehydrated!

All the boys worked hard to finish the farming so that they could go away to the town of Marbel and resume their schooling. Their parents had told them that they had to stay in the farm until all the fields had been planted with rice, corn and some vegetables.

Sal helped out in the clearing of the virgin lands that belonged to his family. His father organized a cooperative sharing of labor. The members of the cooperative donated their work time, tools and work animals to the tilling and planting of rice, corn and vegetables. In time, each member was repaid in kind until all the lands had been planted.

Then, the four older boys, Mabini, Paterno, Hermogenes and Salvador left for Marbel, Cotabato, to enroll in high school. Hermogenes decided to enroll at the Koronadal Public High School as a senior. Mabini and Paterno enrolled as seniors at Notre Dame of Marbel, a Catholic school conducted by the Oblates of Mary Immaculate (OMI) who were American Missionaries. The Oblates were assisted by the Marist Brothers, a teaching order from Boston and by the Sisters of Virgin Mary, a Filipino Order of nuns.

Due to the war interruptions, the three oldest boys found themselves in the same grade after the war. Salvador also enrolled at Notre Dame as a junior. Because he had been "promoted" to higher grades twice, while still illiterate, he found himself just one year behind his older brothers.

The Marist Brothers managed the Boys Department and the Nuns conducted the Girls Department. Even though the sexes were separated in some subjects and activities, the school was coeducational.

Notre Dame was Sal's ideal school! The priests, brothers, nuns and lay teachers were dedicated, inspired and inspiring. For the first time, as a student, he felt very happy being in school! He enjoyed learning literally everything!

For the first time, his grades were hitting the stratosphere! He had received grades as high as 100. He could not believe that any student deserved such grades. In a peculiar way, he was still more comfortable with the grade of 75. His grades were so unreal to him that he didn't tell anyone, not even his parents! Because the grades seemed false, he was afraid they wouldn't hold up and may be changed any time soon!

When he was in his senior year, Mother Maria, the principal of the Girls Department, summoned him to her office.

She said to him smiling broadly, "Salvador, I'm sure you know that you're vying for the highest honors! Let me repeat, the highest honors! This means that you could become the valedictorian. There is only one student who is ahead of you. She is Paquita Demetillo. But she is ahead of you only because of your low grades in first and second years in Mambusao High."

Mother Maria's good news was so shocking to Sal that he kept shaking his head! She could not possibly be talking about him. Salvador was not an honors material! He was an illiterate boy who may not be allowed to graduate from high school!

"Thank you, Mother Maria, for telling me this unexpected and, to me, shocking news! I had absolutely no idea I was in the running for anything. I was just happy to pass my subjects!"

"Tell me, Salvador, why were your grades so low when you were in your first and second years in high school?"

"Reverend Mother, when I was in my first and second years in high school, I was still barely literate. My almost complete isolation during WWII rendered me illiterate after the war. That was incredible even to me! For years, I was failing all my subjects. Even now, I'm not sure whether I'm already literate!"

"How can you doubt your literacy when your grades in English have been straight 99 every grading period? Brother Peter, who teaches the subject, told me that you're the smartest student he had ever taught.

When a person has been walking slowly behind others who naturally walked faster, the slow walker may catch up by increasing the pace but with a great difficulty because walking fast is not part of his nature. After he had caught up and gone ahead, he can stay ahead as long as he maintains the new pace. After maintaining the fast pace for a few years, the new pace becomes part of his nature.

Sal was the slow walker who eventually caught up with his classmates. In fact, as Mother Maria had pointed out, he had already caught up with them but he didn't know it.

One interesting problem that he discovered was that even though he agreed with Mother Maria that he had already gotten ahead of most of his classmates, he couldn't slow down the momentum. It felt more normal to go with the faster pace. The whole struggle of trying to catch up has turned him into an <u>over-achiever</u>! Even today, he wonders whether he can just sit around and enjoy his retirement! Only the future will tell!

One big reason why Sal felt trapped in teaching was because it felt like he was <u>not going anywhere</u>. Going back to the university to work for another doctorate was definitely "going somewhere," which was America!

In December 1965, Sal obtained a student visa and <u>matriculated at New York University</u> to work for a doctorate in education.

His ulterior motives were to be close to his former classmate, Maria Rubio, at Santo Tomas University, who was working for her doctorate in education at Columbia University in Manhattan. He had harbored a secret love for her but never divulged his romantic intentions.

His more important motivation was to find a way to convert his student visa into a permanent residence visa. He had visited the American Embassy in Manila several times and experienced great frustration with the Embassy personnel. The clerks he had talked to repeatedly told him that the Embassy had stopped processing Filipino applications for immigration. They had no idea when the Embassy would resume processing new applications.

Due to the great number of Filipino applicants for immigration, the amount of red tape was so insurmountable that he decided to go to the USA and apply there. He believed that the prospect of obtaining a permanent residence visa through normal channels was very poor.

Because of the dictatorship of Ferdinand Marcos, many Filipinos who opposed his regime, were fleeing the country. Most of them were seeking refuge in America.

He assumed, perhaps wrongly, that being in the USA might enhance his chances of becoming a US resident.

He boarded the President Roosevelt luxury liner in Manila on December 18, 1965 for San Francisco. The passengers, who were mostly bridge players, celebrated the New Year in Hong Kong. The ship stopped over in Tokyo, Yukohama, Guam, Wake Island, Honolulu and arrived in San Francisco on the fourteenth of January 1966. He flew to New York City the next day. He wasted no time to see the woman of his fantasy!

Even though he found Maria very friendly and even coquettish, he was shocked and disappointed to find out that she was already engaged to a Filipino in the Philippines. Maria was going home in six months to get married!

Heartbroken and deeply disillusioned, he tried to find consolation in his studies and research. However, the trick didn't work because he was also suffering from another malady called culture shock! Culture shock is as real as a cold or flu. But, you have to experience it to really know what it feels like. It felt so debilitating, painful and horrible! It was mentally and physically paralyzing!

Culture shock only happens to persons who had been uprooted from their familiar surroundings and from the customs and practices that they were used to. It happens when a person is separated from relatives, friends and from his own people or tribe who were dear to him.

The antidote to culture shock is to plant roots quickly in the new environment, by cultivating new friendships, knowing your new neighbors, familiarizing yourself with the history and culture of your adopted country and by accepting the core values of that country.

Unfortunately, in Greenwich Village, Sal couldn't make friends because almost everyone that he met there was a transient. Almost everyone was keeping a secret, like dodging the draft, being bankrupt, being sought by the police for unpaid child support and many other obligations.

Both photos above were scenes in Washington Square in Greenwich Village, Manhattan

Pol would converse with a person or persons, in Washington Square, for hours and felt that he really knew them. Yet, the next time they met again, he would recognize the persons, who inexplicably acted as if they had never met him before. This phenomenon of "intentional non-recognition" happened several times in the eight months he lived in Greenwich Village.

Because people were hiding something, especially from the government, they purposely wanted to live *incognito*. They didn't want anyone to know or recognize them. For this reason, it was impossible to make friends and he felt completely alienated!

Another scene in Greenwich Village

Coming from a very closely knit community in the Philippines, where people looked at each other's eyes as they greeted, "Good morning," "Good afternoon" or "Good evening," being ignored in Manhattan was cruel, rude and alienating! He noticed that pedestrians purposely didn't look at other people's eyes. Even though he looked at people's faces as he walked around Greenwich Village, he noticed that everyone just looked passed him and gazed at open spaces! It was a weird experience!

In contrast, there was a distinct class of people who looked right into your eyes and were extremely friendly. They were the panhandlers and those with criminal intentions! Understandably,

Sal easily fell for the pseudo-friendships of the panhandlers. They usually had tragic but untrue stories to tell! Within two weeks, Sal was wondering how he could avoid those beggars. For the first time, he understood why New Yorkers avoided looking at people's eyes. They were defending themselves from being swindled by strangers! The look in the eyes was the entry into a person's soul. The eyes that looked back conveyed the message of friendship, peace and welcome. Or, the eyes that looked back may convey the message of anger, hatred and rejection.

The habitués of Greenwich Village were non-committal about what their eyes revealed. By looking into blank spaces, they were delivering a clear message, "Don't talk to me! I have no money to give you!" The evasive behavior prevented the beggars and those with evil intentions from making any headway!

Sal found it difficult not to look at people's faces because it was contrary to his upbringing. Instead, he figured out that if he spoke a language the beggars didn't understand, they would leave him alone! He happened to speak seven of the eighty-seven Philippine dialects. He spoke to them in Tagalog, Ilonggo, Visayan and other vernacular languages. The trick worked beautifully! They had no idea that he understood what they were saying.

After two months, however, he became careless. Instead of using Philippine dialects, he spoke Spanish. Very quickly, he heard mostly Puerto Rican and Mexican accents. He never spoke Spanish again in Manhattan.

****

It took him three months to realize that the transients in Manhattan purposely didn't give true information about who they were and where they came from. Realizing their need for privacy, he gave up and minded his own business! This strategy was wise but self-destructive! In effect, he was rejecting his own upbringing and culture!

Without recognizing it then, he was also suffering from a severe depression! He felt as if there was a fifty pound stone in his chest! The heavy weight he was carrying around made him feel so sad and suicidal!

Nevertheless, there was one small consolation: the semester ended and he received all A's in his courses. He was confident that he could finish his doctorate in two years. He found all his subjects stimulating and challenging!

However, when he registered for the following semester, another shock exploded on his face! He found out with horror that he had only enough money for the registration. He had very little money left to live on! In order to continue his studies, he had to obtain more funds from whatever source.

Unfortunately, he couldn't barrow money from his own family because money was extremely tight. Sal's parents were sending four children to college, at the same time.

He went to the NYU financial aid office, but was told that, as a non-US citizen, he was not qualified for any aid from the university.

Sal was naïve about being a foreigner in a foreign land. For example, he responded to some of the advertisements for summer jobs in the newspaper. He quickly found out that his student visa prohibited him from holding any employment.

In desperation and, as a last resort, he went to the <u>Bureau of Immigration and Naturalization Services</u> to explain his financial situation and to see if there might be a slight chance to convert his student visa into a permanent status.

The female clerk who attended to him told him frankly, "There is absolutely nothing that we can do for you! Every year, thousands of foreign students try to use the same *modus operandi*. They mistakenly assume that being in the country gives them priority over other applicants from their country.

"Let me explain that every country has been assigned a specific quota of potential immigrants to America. Like every other Filipino who wants to immigrate, you should first apply for an immigration visa.

"Frankly, I wouldn't advise you to apply because, right now, there is already a <u>fifteen year waiting period</u> for Filipinos. In other words, the number of Filipinos who have applied has been so large that it will take fifteen years or more to elapse before new quotas will be available to new applicants."

"In that case, I wouldn't bother to apply. I can't wait for fifteen years. I have no idea what my plans will be after fifteen years."

"I understand your point of view. But before you return to your country, I suggest that you see some of the interesting sites in this country, like the famous Niagara Falls in New York State, Colonial Williamsburg in Virginia, the Blue Ridge Parkway that ranges through several states and many others."

"That is a good suggestion. However, I'm very short of cash these days. When I left the Philippines, less than a year ago, I thought I had enough money to study for two years. I had no realistic idea of the cost of living especially here in Manhattan. I should return to my country while I have enough money to pay my plane fare."

"That is probably a wise thing to do. Let me walk you to the door."

Niagara Falls (Canada side)

"It's not necessary. I should find my way out."

"I insist on walking with you because I feel badly for you! You came half a world away to obtain a doctoral degree from NYU.

Instead, you'll be going home empty-handed. It is too bad that you don't have your doctorate yet; because if you do, then I can really help you!"

"Why do you say that? Do you have a special offering for persons with doctorate? I would like to know what it is because I might be already qualified. If you don't mind, please tell me!"

"Yes, I don't mind telling you. There is what is called a Sixth Preference Visa granted to individuals with doctorate degrees. To encourage such individuals to work in the United States, we process their applications immediately and quickly."

"Does the doctorate have to be obtained from a US university?"

"No. It can be from any accredited university anywhere in the world. It could be from the University of Timbuktu, for all I know. I'm just kidding; I don't know if there is a University of Timbuktu. I don't even know where Timbuktu is!"

"Timbuktu is a town in central Mali, in West Africa, near the Niger River."

"To me, Timbuktu is any far away place. I didn't know that it even existed."

"Just to get back to my line of questioning, would a doctorate in the humanities qualify?"

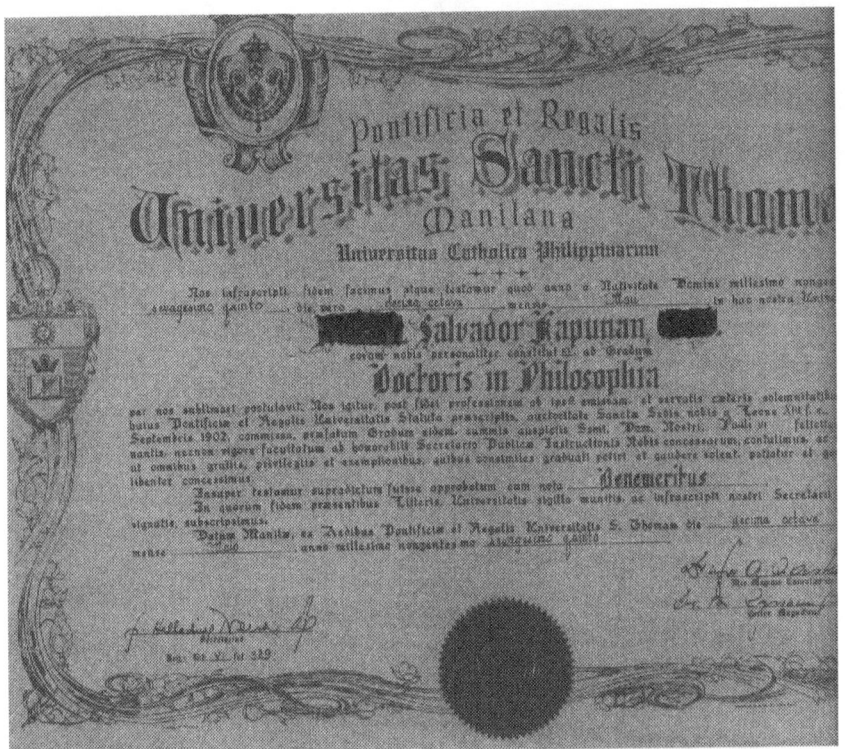

The applicant's doctoral diploma from the University of Santo Tomas, Manila, Philippines

"It certainly would! A doctorate is a doctorate, whatever the field."

"In that case, I'll come back tomorrow because I already have a doctorate in philosophy from the University of Santo Tomas in Manila."

"You already have a Ph.D. in philosophy? Why bother to acquire a doctorate in education, if I may ask?"

"I agree it sounds superfluous; but I have my own reasons that are difficult to explain to others."

"That's fine with me; it is really none of my business. Come back whenever you want. You don't have to ask for me. Anyone here can process your application. Congratulations for this unexpected change of events!"

"Thank you so much. You really helped me without intending to. When I left the Philippines, somehow I had the hunch that my doctorate in philosophy would open some doors. Now, my hunch has already come to fruition because America has invited me in because I have a doctorate in philosophy! I had no idea that a doctorate has that kind of value and power!"

"That's for sure! Some people are luckier than others! This is the first time I've watched one's fortunes changed right before my eyes!"

"Thank you so much for the help. I would like to ask another question."

"Go ahead and ask."

"You explained earlier that there is a fifteen year waiting period for Filipinos applying for a US immigration visa. Is that the reason why the US Embassy in Manila had stopped processing applications for US immigration?"

"Yes. That is the reason."

"I find it amazing that I have to come all the way to America to find out why the application for immigration to this country was discontinued in Manila."

"Yes. It is interesting. But, did you ask that question in Manila?"

"Yes. I did but nobody knew the reasons."

****

The next day, Sal brought his doctoral diploma and all the supporting documents. He filled out his application form and in a few short minutes, he had his "green card" that allowed him to apply for any job anywhere in the United States and her territories.

His "green card" validated his assumption that he would live a more free life by immigrating to the United States. His possibilities seemed infinite! He didn't have to teach to make a living. He could choose to be a business man and sell fish from a push cart. While many options were available, he had already invested ten years of his life to acquire a Ph.D. in philosophy so he could teach philosophy in a college or a university. It seemed wise to pursue a teaching career in philosophy as a starting point of his new life. Later on, he may find another field that is more interesting and more lucrative.

Since he had already taught philosophy at a university level for five years, he felt he should find out if he could find another teaching position in philosophy any where in the USA.

****

He bought a portable typewriter and composed his resume. He selected twenty small colleges and universities in the eastern seaboard and sent inquiries about a teaching position in philosophy. In two weeks, he received a response from Dr. James Claghorn, chairman of the philosophy department of West Chester State College in Pennsylvania, near Philadelphia. Dr. Claghorn invited him to visit the college campus for an interview and meet the other faculty members.

Sal got the job because of the recommendations of Dr. Julio Bravo, a Filipino-American professor of biology at the same college. Dr. Bravo had attended Santo Tomas University for four years for his undergraduate degree in biology. He also immigrated to America in order to pursue his doctorate in science.

Dr. Bravo told Dr. Claghorn that Santo Tomas was in the same caliber as Harvard University. He might have exaggerated the educational caliber of Santo Tomas a little bit but it helped Sal secure the job.

Sal's starting salary in July 1966 was only $6,910 for the nine month academic term. If he taught courses for the summer sessions, he could earn an additional $3000. He was single and he thought that his salary was a lot of money. His meager salary was, in fact, ten times more than what he made in the Philippines.

The West Chester College band playing on July 4th

Being a new immigrant didn't prepare him for dealing with racial discrimination. Accompanied by Dr. Claghorn, Sal applied to rent an apartment from a white female property manager in the city of West Chester. The property manager kept suggesting that he should rent a trailer inside a trailer park. Dr. Claghorn strongly vetoed the suggestion; that a trailer living wasn't appropriate for a college professor.

They looked at two different apartments: a one bedroom and an efficiency apartment. Sal chose a one bedroom, which rented for $300 a month. He made a $100 deposit to secure it for two weeks. He promised to pay the first month's rent and the security deposit when he signed the lease in two weeks.

When he returned two weeks later, there was no record of his application and the woman who took his deposit wasn't available. When he demanded the return of his deposit, the attending personnel refused to make the refund on the grounds that there was no record of the transaction. The office manager didn't issue him a receipt.

He conferred with Dr. Claghorn about the mishandling of his application. Claghorn apologized for the unfair incident. He suspected that there was an <u>internal discriminatory policy</u>, which was known only to company personnel, that limited the renters to white clients only. In order to expose the discrimination, Sal would have to hire a lawyer and sue the owners and managers of the apartment buildings.

Sal balked at his suggestion to sue. He didn't want to start his career in America with a lawsuit. Even if he won, he was afraid of retaliation. He knew nothing about the city; he needed to keep a low profile! However, he was optimistic that he would find a suitable housing soon. Meanwhile, he was residing in an old hotel that had already been scheduled for demolition.

Two days later, he was eating breakfast in a small eatery on Market St in West Chester. The owner of a beauty shop, across the street, was also eating breakfast.

Mrs. Helen Bradford said to Sal, "Are you still looking for an apartment? I have a one bedroom unit across the street that is available immediately. The apartment is on the second floor, above my beauty shop."

Even though he had never talked to her before, he automatically said, "Yes! I do need an apartment. I can move in today. How much is the rent?"

"It will be seventy-five dollars a month. I require the first month's rent and a security deposit."

"No problem. May I see it first?"

"Go over to the beauty shop across the street when you're ready and I'll show it to you."

He lived there for four years. Helen Bradford, the beautician, turned out to be a wonderful landlady. Obviously, Helen mistook Sal for another Oriental who was also looking for an apartment. Those were among the vicissitudes of fortune among people who looked alike! With some nice people living in West Chester, like Helen Bradford, the other Oriental would also have a nice lodging.

Interestingly, his <u>depression</u> suddenly lifted! He was no longer carrying the fifty pound weight in his chest! He was walking around the campus grinning from ear to ear like a fool! People stopped and stared at him but he didn't mind it. He was giddy with joy because, unexpectedly, he became a permanent resident of the United States; he had a good job, a wonderful apartment and wasn't depressed anymore! He was happy beyond his greatest expectations!

Chapter Two.
Making Philosophy Relevant

Sal loved teaching undergraduate students. There was a certain innocence and natural curiosity about them. When he was teaching in the Philippines, he taught seven classes and made four separate class preparations. At West Chester State, he was teaching only four classes a day and was making only two class preparations.

Professor Kapunan

In the beginning, some of the students had problems with his Filipino accent. He tried to figure out what specific problems they were experiencing and what he could do about it.

He realized that the primary problem was in the pronunciation or non-pronunciation of the letter "h." Somehow, like most Filipinos, the "h" was hardly pronounced. Often, words like "the" sounded like "de" and "those" sounded like "dose".

On the second week of his teaching, he said to each of his classes, "Listen class, I know I have an accent, which was really shocking to me because before I came to this country, I spoke good English. I attended an excellent private school in Manila, with a very high standard of education. Ninety percent of my teachers were American educators. Suddenly, upon arriving in this country, I immediately acquired a foreign accent called 'Filipino.'

"Let me point out where my problems are and perhaps you'll understand me better. I'm not able to pronounce the letter 'h,' in "the," "those," "that" and many other words. It goes without saying that I'll try harder to pronounce my letter "h" from now on."

His own analysis of his foreign accent seemed to help the students. At every class, he handed out copies of his <u>typed notes</u> that underscored the important ideas and topics that he had covered. The notes plus the textbooks and class discussions facilitated the learning process.

Sal knew that philosophic subjects could be very interesting to students who liked <u>abstract thinking</u>. Unfortunately, in any group, there were students who preferred visual learning. For instance, a student approached him privately and said, "Instead of just lecturing, don't you think the classes would be more interesting if you showed us movies, instead?"

Sal was speechless! After he had recovered, he said simply, "I'm sorry that I don't know any movies that would teach the lessons I'm trying to teach in my classes. However, if you know of such movies, let me know and I'll be glad to project them on a screen."

He noticed, at the next class, that the student was absent; he suspected that he had dropped out of the course. It was somewhat of a relief for him; but, at the same time, he also felt like a failure. He was trying his best. Obviously, he couldn't win everyone!

He had to admit that many of the philosophic concepts he was discussing in class had no practical applications for some students. He was aware that what were important to them were ideas and lessons that could help them in their careers and in their personal lives!

In response to these concerns, he said to his classes, "In order to make philosophy relevant to your lives, I'll teach you <u>logical reasoning</u> and <u>critical thinking starting in two weeks</u>. Whatever your chosen field maybe, you will always need to use logical and critical thinking. In fact, you'll need these philosophic skills in your daily lives.

"Hence, I will teach you the fundamentals of <u>inductive and deductive reasoning</u>. I will also teach you how to be critical of your own thinking. Don't ask me now what inductive or deductive reasoning means. I'll make sure that you understand these important concepts before the semester is over."

After teaching them logical and critical thinking, they had a better appreciation of philosophy. They realized that philosophy was indeed relevant and important in their lives!

****

Teaching in college during the 1960s and 70s was full of anxiety, fear and confusion for the college students and for some professors as well. There was a <u>cultural revolution</u> going on, which had profound effects on the lives of the students! The young, especially the college students, were questioning the validity of the existing values and the fundamental principles of their society!

There were different kinds of movements going on: racial equality, gender equality, the civil rights movement in the south, the right not to serve in Vietnam based on one's conscience and so on. The widening opposition to the Vietnam War gave the political activists greater courage and confidence to disrupt the existing order of the American society! Political protests some times led to some violent riots!

Some students and political groups even took over college campuses and made <u>non-negotiable demands</u>. The non-negotiable demands frustrated and intimidated the school administrators and purposely called attention to the protester's causes. By disrupting legitimate school meetings and activities, the protesters were sending the message that they were in control!

One day, West Chester College invited a representative of the South Vietnamese government to speak on political matters occurring in South Vietnam. He wasn't able to speak at all! Every time he attempted to speak, some students and professors in the audience drowned him out by yelling, "Booooo!" They also used paddles and musical instruments to create prolonged noise that drowned out the speaker's voice!

The West Chester State students were not actively involved in violent protests. However, they were interested in discussing the issues underscored by the protesters.

There were two older male students on campus who were agitating for various changes at West Chester State campus. According to some professors Sal had talked to, the older students were not formally enrolled in the college. They were only auditing some classes in political science. The prevalent rumor was that they were members of the National Communists Party. They were organizing different cells on various college campuses in Pennsylvania, New Jersey, Maryland and neighboring states for organized protests.

Sal saw the need for a moderated discussion of the issues! In order to promote greater understanding of the various contemporary problems, Sal obtained permission to use the college auditorium for a weekly moderated debate or open discussion of the disputed issues. Initially, he acted as the moderator and invited student leaders, faculty members and college administrators to the discussions. The two auditing students became extremely active in his discussion group, which he called The Open Forum.

In retrospect, the new discussion group provided a new outlet and opportunity for the cell recruiters to proselytize for the cells they were forming.

From Sal's point of view, however, he thought he was doing the college a favor. Unfortunately, the administration was becoming uncomfortable, defensive and nervous, fearing that violence might happen, sooner or later! Every time Sal invited some board members to appear on a panel, they simply ignored the invitation. Still, he continued to conduct open discussions, without any input from the administration.

Sal started to wonder whether the administration had placed him in the company of the agitators. Before long, he found out that some administrators had labeled him as a campus activist. It was true that the two agitators were active in his discussion group but he didn't recruit them. Still, his incidental association with the cell recruiters was like a kiss of death! He foresaw that he wouldn't get his tenure and might be asked to resign from teaching!

To ease off the heat from him, he asked other faculty members to act as moderators. However, his attempt to distance himself from the agitators didn't help. Some powerful administrators wanted Kapunan out of West Chester State as soon as possible!

After four years of teaching, Dr. Claghorn formally asked him to resign from teaching in West Chester. The chairman even threatened him that if he didn't resign, the <u>Bureau of Immigration and Naturalization Services</u> might investigate his activities on campus. Sal knew he was innocent and welcomed the BINS investigation. He knew that the threat was only an intimidation tactic!

His friends and supporters urged him to fight the dismissal. On the other hand, he was afraid that if he contested being denied tenure, his cause could polarize the whole college! The philosophy department had some unstable and hot-headed students who could disrupt the campus! They were looking for a strong cause as a vehicle to promote the changes that they were demanding from the administration.

At that time, the students were demanding freedom to show romantic gestures to their sweethearts in public. Some prudish faculty members habitually walked around the campus and openly chided couples who were holding hands or kissing.

They were also demanding to wear informal clothes to eat meals at the cafeteria. They found it ridiculous to dress in jackets and high heels just to eat the insipid cafeteria glop!

Above all, they were demanding that curfew hours be abolished for weekends! The existing rule was that dormitory residents had to be in by midnight even on weekends.

****

After pondering hard on the risks and the costs of a lengthy litigation, Sal decided to send in <u>his resignation</u>! By leaving West Chester State, he could pursue other avenues and travel to more interesting places.

He decided to use the hiatus to go back to the university to finish his <u>doctorate in education</u>. He had the hunch that an American doctorate would be useful for his economic survival in America. Unfortunately, he had very little savings because he was sending money to his parents every month to help them maintain their life style and to help them with their expensive medications.

The only way for him to go back to the university was if an institution offered him some kind of <u>scholarship</u>.

He applied for scholarship to the University of Pennsylvania and to Temple University in Philadelphia. The University of Penn just ignored his application. The fact was that he never received a reply or an explicit rejection.

Fortunately, <u>Temple University offered him a $6,000 fellowship</u>, without any obligations, except to formally matriculate at the university. He registered in the <u>Foundations of Education Department</u> and had a full load of four courses per semester. Even though he already had a Ph.D. in philosophy, it would still take him two full years to cover all the required courses for a doctorate in Foundations of Education.

He made a resolve to finish his research, write his doctoral dissertation and finish all his courses in two years! Most doctoral candidates take at least three years to finish their doctorate.

The reason why Sal majored in Foundations of Education was due to the specialties of the faculty members and the emphasis of the whole department in the use of *linguistic analysis*. Linguistic analysis is the art and the science of isolating the primary concepts of any discipline and analyzing the logical implications of each concept.

Sal planned to apply the linguistic analysis techniques especially to the most central concepts of education, which are <u>teaching</u> and <u>learning</u>. He had already decided on the title of his doctoral dissertation. It would be: <u>The Task and Achievement Senses of Teaching and Learning.</u>

He asked Dr. Paul Komisar, who was then the Department Chairman, to be his dissertation adviser. Komisar gladly accepted the responsibility.

He received his doctorate in May 1973, exactly two years after he started his doctorate. His doctoral diploma is photo-copied below.

TEMPLE · UNIVERSI1

OF·THE·COMMONWEALTH·SYSTEM·OF·HIGHER·EDUCATI

BY·AUTHORITY·OF·THE·BOARD·OF·TRUSTEES·AND·UPON·RECOMM

OF·THE·FACULTY·HEREBY·CONFERS·UPON

~ Salvador C. Kapunan ~

THE · DEGREE · OF

Doctor of Education

TOGETHER·WITH·ALL·THE·RIGHTS·PRIVILEGES·AND·HONORS·APPI

THERETO · IN · RECOGNITION · OF · THE · SATISFACTORY · COI

OF · THE · COURSE · PRESCRIBED · BY · THE · FACULTY · OF · THE · UI

IN · TESTIMONY · WHEREOF · THE · UNDERSIGNED · HAVE · SUI

THEIR · NAMES · AND · AFFIXED · THE · SEAL · OF · THE · UNI

GIVEN · AT · PHILADELPHIA · PENNSYLVANIA · ON · THIS · TWENTY·

OF · MAY · NINETEEN · HUNDRED · AND · SEVENTY · THREE

Doctor of Education Diploma

Sal didn't attend his graduation. Perhaps, his lack of enthusiasm was indicative of the economic recession that was already going on in the country. He knew that finding a full time job at the time was nearly impossible. He merely went to the registrar's office to pick up his diploma.

He suspected that <u>employment in the Philippines</u> might be better. He was still a citizen of the Philippines. In July, 1973, he made a trip to the Philippines and made inquiries about a full-time job in the City of Cebu and in Manila.

The <u>University of Cebu</u> offered him a full-time job but the conditions were not acceptable to him. He would have to teach seven different subjects, act as adviser to all doctoral students and there was no possibility of acquiring a tenured position. Tenure was reserved only for administrators. Strictly speaking, professors in the Philippines held only part-time jobs. This part-time status explained why there was <u>no tenure</u> for them.

Sal found out that those who taught at the college or university levels in the Philippines were actual practitioners in their fields. Hence, law professors were judges and prominent trial lawyers. Those who taught medicine were physicians with a large medical practice.

Theoretically, this part-time way of staffing classrooms was better than hiring full-time professors. However, the primary rationale for this policy was economics. It costs much less to hire part-time professors because they had no benefits. They were paid by the number of courses they taught. They might not even have an office where they could meet their students.

Part-time teaching was practiced all over the country. Hence, there was no need to inquire further from the other universities.

Under those conditions, Sal decided to reject the offer and returned to Philadelphia. He decided to wait until something opened up in his field somewhere in the USA. He also figured out that teaching part-time in the USA was better than teaching full-time in a country that paid its employees "starvation wages." He knew what it meant to teach seven different classes in the Philippines because he had done that for five years. Five years of teaching seven courses burned him out! That was one reason why he immigrated to America.

Upon his return to Philadelphia, his first priority was to <u>become a US citizen</u>. Becoming a citizen would preclude useless and costly trips to his motherland. The brief visit to the Philippines made him realize that he had become too Americanized and would never be comfortable with the old culture again. During the whole month that he lived in the Philippines, he felt suffocated by all the problems of his family and relatives. They assumed that every America was rich and generous! Even children aggressively asked for "dollars!"

To make the change complete, he <u>changed his name</u> to Leopoldo (Pol) Mabulbul.

In order to support himself, he accepted a part-time employment at La Salle College in Philadelphia. He taught philosophical and sociological foundations of education.

In the fall of 1976, he accepted another part-time employment at Temple University, his alma mater. He was teaching three courses in Foundations of Education.

****

Unfortunately, there were strong credible rumors that the department of Foundations of Education might be phased out because of the declining enrollment in the college of education. Pol ignored the rumors and applied himself to his new position.

He was only glad to have a job at the time when factory workers were being laid off by the thousands every day. The recession of the 1980s was very severe! Short term interest rates had gone up to 22%. Banks were not lending any money and the economy was virtually paralyzed!

The severe recession was brought about by rising inflation that started in 1969 and lasted into the 1980s. The inflation peaked at 13 percent in 1980. In 1981, the monthly unemployment rate was 10.8 percent. The high interest rates were the Federal Government's attempt to control the run-away inflation.

Under those economic conditions, it was scary to try anything new! And yet, workers were being dismissed by the thousands every day! Fear was in the air especially for a new citizen like Pol! His future was suddenly uncertain! The economic conditions would get worse for at least four years before they would get better!

Nevertheless, Pol was determined to survive at whatever level he could! He knew that the economy was cyclical and it would turn around again! When the new economic cycle comes around, there would be new opportunities to start a new prosperous life! Becoming a US citizen positioned himself to take advantage of new opportunities!

Chapter Three.
Tying the Matrimonial Knot

During the summer of 1978, Pol happened to meet a lovely woman who had been recently widowed. She was a charming American Jew named, Yeta Markowitz.

Yeta Markowitz as a young woman

Pol had dated younger women of various nationalities. She was by far the most compatible with his character and personality.

She was actually older than him by four years. He realized that dating someone close to his age was more comfortable, relaxing and natural!

On the other hand, Yeta suspected that he might be too young for her. She estimated that he could be as young as twenty-five and as old as forty. She always had problems estimating the age of Orientals because they often came out older than they looked.

In order to ascertain his age, she solicited her neighbor's help. She asked Rhoda to ask him, "How old were you when you came to this country?" Then, she should ask some time later, "When did you come to this country?"

Yeta and Pol in the Bubble Room in Captiva, Fl.

Unfortunately, Pol derailed the line of questioning by saying, "Aha! You're trying to find out how old I am. I'll save you the trouble. I was 45 as of last June."

Having put aside the subject of age, they started to bond immediately! The tegmental area and the caudate nucleus of their brains were glowing brightly! Those areas of the brain are home to a dense spread of receptors for neurotransmitters called dopamine, which were their <u>endogenous love potions</u>! The dopamine flow was just right and it created intense energy, exhilaration, focused attention and the motivation to bond!

They conversed for several hours deep into the night and could never finish any topic! As a middle-aged man, for the first time, he was instantly in love! Because he was actually experiencing <u>being in love</u>, for the first time, he finally understood what love really meant!

Before meeting Yeta, love to him was a Western fictional concept that writers merely imagined. He didn't believe in it simply because he had never experienced it. He had dated extensively and had been engaged three times to three different women but he didn't experience love. What he had experienced was lust, not love. What he experienced with Yeta was spontaneous and the relationship had a life of its own! Sometimes, they felt like spectators to what was happening between them. However, very often they spontaneously acted on how they felt!

****

Yeta was a highly accomplished professional, with a degree in psychology and worked in that field for several years. However, like many American professionals who were also housewives and mothers, she had shifted her career as she raised her three children. Meanwhile, she also acquired a degree in interior design.

She had worked as a radio producer for the Public Broadcasting Station in Philadelphia for many years. She also produced her own radio program called, "Open to the Public," in which she interviewed celebrities and ordinary but interesting personalities.

She had also worked as an artistic director of a *Theater Arts for Youth*, a non-profit organization that produced plays for children and young adults. She was the most interesting woman Pol had ever met!

****

They started dating in June 1978 and both realized that their relationship was moving fast to what was inevitable: marriage!

Yet, Pol was purposely applying breaks at every turn to slow down the progress of the relationship because he had vowed never to get married only five years earlier!

He had dated young women, half his age, because he wanted to have children. However, the more he reflected on raising children and how much it would cost, the more he realized that he was too old to be a father. He was already in his forties.

He also realized that he was not a good candidate for marriage because he was too set in his ways! Having lived alone for so long, it would be impossible to live with another person, let alone with a woman!

At age forty five and faced with the prospect of marriage, Pol <u>became a bundle of contradictions</u>! Since meeting Yeta, he kept vacillating between wanting to remain single and carefree and, at the same time, feeling tantalized by the unknown, which promised life-transforming romance and unending happiness!

He knew that he was always obsessed by women. He reasoned that the natural attraction was energized by the natural drive to procreate. He loved women and truly enjoyed their company. In fact, he enjoyed talking to women more than talking to men. Very often, he found talking to men unsatisfactory and frustrating.

With very few exceptions, men didn't give him the whole truth or the whole picture! They seemed to withhold some important information in order to impress or mislead him. This tendency to play their cards close to the vests was probably due to the fierce competition among them. He suspected that men were playing some games that he didn't understand. And, when it came to feelings, men came across as robots.

On the other hand, women gave him more information than he cared to know. The women he knew seemed to relish the process of baring their souls to him. Without doubt, the female gender had no trouble giving everyone the whole picture. Women seemed to be saying, "What you see is what you get."

If a man didn't get a clear message, women have no problem explaining the same things a thousand times more! From about the age of two or three, boys noticed that girls could out-talk them to tears! The verbal gap actually gets worse as they age because having discovered that their forte is language, the female gender always exploits this advantage! Who could blame them? Pol certainly would not! In fact, one of the reasons why he admired the fairer sex was their verbal facility!

Yet, Pol was afraid to commit himself to something serious as marriage! This fear was exacerbated by his promise to himself not to get married.

Given the existing resolve not to get married, he tried to clarify to himself what the necessary and sufficient conditions were for him to change his mind.

First of all, he stipulated that the first condition was that <u>Yeta must truly love him,</u> in spite of his shortcomings. He was virtually a poor man since he was working only part-time. He couldn't take her to fancy restaurants or give her expensive gifts.

In spite of being from the Philippines where people often married without factoring in *love* into the equation, Pol believed that love was a potent force that could bind the lovers into one, even in sickness and in pain!

Spike Gillespie wrote an article in the NY Times entitled, "Modern Love." She underscored some concepts that Pol could empathize with. She wrote, "The things we all want, the most simple and elusive thing in the world: to be and feel truly, deeply loved, and to share that love with equal depth." Pol knew that he shared the same deep feelings of love with Yeta!

The second condition was that <u>she wouldn't want more children</u> than the three she already had. He found out that she couldn't have more children even if she wanted to. She had a hysterectomy a few years earlier.

The next conditions were that <u>she must love sex</u>; that she was <u>not a drug addict</u>; that she was <u>pretty</u>; <u>monogamous, independent-minded</u> and a <u>feminist.</u>

Since Yeta met all these conditions, he was romantically hooked! He had no more excuses!

Slowly, he was changing his position every day and enjoyed the romantic ride! Every day, he imagined what it meant to live as a married man, for the first time, and married to the cute and beautiful

Yeta! He had to admit that she was a good cook, a good friend and a very good companion!

By November 1978, he knew that they would set a date for their wedding. Yeta set it for January 4, 1979.

Surrounded by friends and the immediate family, they tied the conjugal knot before a judge in the City Hall of Philadelphia as scheduled. They honeymooned in Cancun, Mexico and became a very happy couple!

The Bride and Groom

Yeta's family: daughters Candi and Stephanie, younger brother, Murray and sister-in-law, Elaine and nephew, Ken

With Pol's cousin Ruby and Popoy

The wedding reception at a restaurant

****

Inevitably, some problems surfaced in their marriage that Pol didn't expect! Because Yeta had been married for over twenty years, she had an existing social baggage that Pol didn't want to carry on his shoulders! All her friends were also the friends of her late husband, Sheldon. Out of respect and loyalty to Sheldon, some of her friends were openly hostile to Pol! Some were outright rejecting and made remarks that implied that Pol was an intruder and a complete outsider.

He suspected that they were trying to poison the relationship! Before the wedding, some were openly opposed to the marriage on the assumption that Pol would only break Yeta's heart! Some pointed out that a man in his forties who had not been married, could never adjust to a married life and would soon leave the relationship!

Even those who were accepting, also unintentionally excluded him. Because of the long history of their friendships, much of what they talked about was completely unfamiliar to Pol. He was literally a stranger looking in. The constant references to Sheldon made Pol resent him! He suspected that the frequent references to Sheldon were their way of affirming their friendship and affection for him, even though he was no longer around.

One night, however, Pol had a <u>didactic dream</u> that straightened out his thinking. In the dream, he vividly observed Sheldon walking down the spiral staircase from his residence in the attic of 216 Delhi St! He walked all the way down to the basement, where the kitchen was situated. He looked around and looked at Yeta and Pol but said nothing.

Pol knew, even in his dream, that Sheldon was not a living person; nevertheless, he still lived with them in the attic of their house.

When he woke up, he knew what the dream meant. It signified that Sheldon would always live with them because he was part of Yeta's life and consciousness. Sheldon would always be part of their lives, as if he lived with them on Delhi St. He also understood that he must accept Yeta and all her circumstances: children, relatives, friends and acquaintances, even those he truly disliked!

After he had accepted Yeta's complete reality and made the necessary mental adjustments, Sheldon didn't have to walk down the staircase again.

For two people who were born and raised half a world apart, their improvable marriage has been extremely happy! The major credit has to be attributed to Yeta! Because of her long experience as a successful married woman, she knew what adjustments needed to be made for the relationship to run smoothly.

She told him what her needs were: she wanted to eat out at least once a week; she wanted to see a movie once a week; go to a play or theater once a month and to travel somewhere once every two or three months. Since her demands were reasonable, there has been very little friction.

Pol, too, had his needs. He didn't like to wake up early. He wanted to go to sleep late, around 11:30 PM. He liked to drink a small glass of liquor as an inducement to sleep. He knew that this practice was frowned upon by physicians, who didn't know everything. He wanted to be alone to think, analyze ideas, contemplate, meditate and read the newspaper and selected books during the day. He was free to converse or watch the television with Yeta in the evenings.

A few years later, because of divergent interests, each one watched his or her programs in different rooms. Yeta preferred to watch light programs, comedies and interesting movies by using the television set in the living room.

Pol wanted to watch the history channel, the discovery and the learning channels. He also liked to watch the National Geographic, the travel channels and sports channels. He preferred to watch his programs in his large bedroom, where he has a desk and a laptop computer.

At around 10:30 or eleven in the evening, they watched together a comedy program like "All in the Family," "The Golden Girls," "Roseanne," "Three's a Company," "The Cosby Show," "Becker" or "Andy Griffith." Watching a comic show prepares and relaxes them for sleep.

Because Pol snored almost every night, both found it convenient and practical to sleep in different bedrooms. Initially, Yeta felt that her new husband was rejecting her. After two weeks of sleeping apart, she realized that she truly liked the new arrangement.

The only altercation that was worth noting happened when they were still courting. Yeta's sister-in-law, Elaine, noted that even though she like Pol a lot, Yeta ought to upgrade some of his old-fashioned clothes. Yeta told Pol about Elaine's remark and he responded by saying, "I authorize you to throw away any clothes that you think should have been given away to Good Will years ago."

For about twenty minutes, Yeta threw away boxes of outdated clothes. Pol felt relieved to part from clothes he hadn't worn in years. Unfortunately, it was already about one in the afternoon and Pol was feeling hungry. He knew that hunger made him irritable. So, he implored her to go out and eat lunch. But, Yeta said, "There is just a little more to do. Just give me about ten more minutes."

While Pol was trying to control his hunger, Yeta suddenly threw away some of his favorite suits. Among the clothes she threw away was a new green golf sweater, which he liked very much.

Uncontrollably, Pol yelled, "Why are you throwing away perfectly good suits and clothes that cost me hundreds of dollars? You have no right to throw away my good clothes! This is an invasion and violation of my property!"

"Pol, what is really wrong? I thought I was doing you a favor. You authorized me to do this and now you're angry with me. What is wrong? Are you trying to break our engagement?"

"I'm sorry, Yeta, I lost my temper! It happens when I'm very hungry. Perhaps my blood sugar had dropped severely. Let us go out and eat something. I'm sure I'll regain my control when I'm no longer hungry."

Sure enough, after lunch, Pol saw Yeta's point of view. She discarded the green sweater because, according to her, the color didn't go with his skin. <u>Green made him look yellow</u>!

Pol suspected that the wearing of green clothes among the Chinese and other Oriental countries gave the illusion of the so-called "yellow race." He had never seen people who had yellow skin. He himself was partly Chinese. So, Yeta was right. From some angles, with the sun light just shinning in a special way on his green sweater, he must have looked yellow!

The yellow race was an optical illusion from looking at green clothes. It was an interesting legend!

Pol allowed Yeta to throw away whatever she didn't like and reduced his wardrobe to only a quarter of what he had owned.

After their wedding, she bought for him new casual clothes, like jeans, which he had despised as clothes for laborers, gangsters and cowboys. After he wore his first jeans, he came down from his pedestal and, for the first time, he felt like a normal happy human being! In fact, he didn't mind looking yellow at all!

"The yellow race is an optical illusion caused by the wearing of green clothes on sunny days in many areas in the Orient but especially in China."

Yeta Markowitz

Chapter Four.
Running Out of Options

Pol worked hard to obtain a second doctorate so he would have more options in teaching. He had a naïve assumption that life for him was nothing more than teaching at the college or university level. He could teach courses in philosophy or in education. He couldn't envision any other life!

In spite of his naivety, he could sense that jobs in philosophy were very difficult to find especially in secular institutions. There were jobs in philosophy in religious colleges but the jobs also called for teaching religious courses. He didn't relish the combination.

One day, he heard over the radio that a college in Spain simply phased out its philosophy department. He thought that it was odd that a country that was traditionally sympathetic to liberal arts would close its doors to philosophy.

College curricula in America were becoming more work-oriented and philosophy was generally viewed as irrelevant to the modern curricula. In 1980, Foundations of Education was also becoming irrelevant.

Fortunately, he had a part-time teaching position at Temple University. But, he knew that the enrollment in the college of education had gone down drastically. There was a credible rumor that the Foundations of Education Department, with ten faculty members, would be phased out sometime in the future. Perhaps, one or two faculty members would be reassigned to the Elementary or Secondary Education. Nobody knew who would be fired or retained!

There was a vicious jockeying for position among those who were hoping to be retained. All the eight senior faculty members were lobbying the influential administrators. For the sake of academic and economic survival, the faculty members were poised to slander or even harm each other physically. They were clawing at each other's character and personality traits. It was ugly and disgusting to observe. Pol didn't want to be part of the chaotic and charged atmosphere in the department!

To make matters literally worse, a senior faculty caught a graduate student altering his grades in the records office. Since the student had no normal access to the records department, someone in that department must have lent him the keys. The student refused to implicate his collaborators. The professor of Historical Foundations of Education was determined to get to the bottom of the scandal. He intended to impress the administration of his usefulness by solving the scandal quickly and quietly.

In his simplistic attempt to foil the professor's efforts, the graduate student bought a hand gun and threatened to shoot the teacher. The next day, the professor also bought a larger caliber revolver to scare off the student!

There was a lot of anger and fear drifting, like marijuana smoke, from one office to another. Every day, new rumors were going around! For example, there was a rumor that the faculty involved with the grades tampering was recruiting three or four other faculty members to form a faction! Then, there was another rumor that the graduate student had also won the allegiance of some faculty members from other departments! Then, there was another vicious rumor that each faction was arming themselves for some kind of battle to be agree upon by the members!

So as not to get caught in a cross fire, Pol wanted to resign immediately! But Peter Goldstone, the acting chairman, persuaded him to wait until the end of the semester. Predictably, he would be gone from teaching by the end of the semester and may never return!

The conflicts, machinations and intrigues in the department probably hastened the phasing out of the department. The following semester, even tenured professors were asked to resign immediately! Two professors were retained: one for Elementary Education Department and another for Secondary Education.

Two tenured professors sued the University for violating the tenure system but lost their cases! It was difficult to justify legally and economically an academic tenure in the face of a reduced student enrollment and severe budget cuts!

The actual causes of the closure of the Foundations of Education Department were a chain of demographic phenomena. Throughout the country, fewer pupils were enrolled in the elementary schools. As a result, there were also fewer pupils enrolled in the middle schools and in high schools. With fewer students to service, some teachers were asked to resign and, understandably, <u>no new teachers were being hired</u>.

At the college level, students who were majoring in education quickly abandoned their specialty and hastily shifted to other fields where there were better prospects of being employed.

When Pol understood the <u>national scope of the problem</u>, he knew it was time to abandon the sinking ship! He knew that he was wasting years of professional training in two disciplines, but he had to face the new realities! .He must find another line of work outside of the academia.

Unfortunately, Yeta was also jobless! Both of them were only in their forties and they couldn't afford to retire yet.

As a middle-aged couple, they had to <u>start all over again</u>, which was very difficult to do! There were no words in the English language that could describe their state of shock and confusion! They were mentally paralyzed for a while because their <u>future was suddenly uncertain</u>! Their new marriage was also threatened! The lack or shortage of money was a divisive factor!

They looked at different retail businesses but their primary obstacle was <u>lack of capital</u>. They had <u>no savings.</u> Theoretically, they were willing to consider any type of work, however menial it maybe!

Pol immediately realized that <u>menial work was a prohibited territory</u>! Six years earlier when he couldn't find a teaching position, he applied for any work being advertised in his attempt to survive financially. For example, there were several advertisements for pest extermination. He knew that any moron could kill bugs.

He made appointments for interview. He knew the interviewer would question him about his educational background. He prepared a very brief resume that omitted all his advanced academic degrees.

Every interviewer figured out that he was hiding something that they wanted to know. *They wanted to know whether he belonged to the working class.* They found out that he belonged to the academic class, a highly sheltered group with advanced academic degrees. After admitting his camouflage and a harmless lie, they vented their anger at him!

"You are here on false pretenses!" an interviewer bellowed! "You have wasted my time. There is no way I would hire you. We spend good money to train our employees. Good training is part of our investments. If we trained you, we would be wasting money because you will leave the job as soon as an opening comes up in your specialty!"

Pol couldn't gainsay their arguments. Truthfully, he had no intention of spending the rest of his life killing bugs. They had a good point. <u>Modern society is made up of specialists</u>. He had to find a job in his specialty. If there were no jobs open, for the time being, he must wait patiently until an opening comes up. Or, what was even better, he must <u>create his own unique specialty and create his own job too!</u>

So, both Yeta and Pol dismissed the whole world of menial jobs and were about to create their own brand of expertise, whatever it maybe! All they were trying to do was survive in America, the land of all kinds of opportunities! Filled with uncertainty, still they felt confident that they would <u>find a way to survive together</u>! Together, they would start a new life and <u>recreate themselves!</u> They must form a new vision and find a niche, without displacing anyone!

Luckily, the subject of real estate investments was paramount in the papers, radio and television. There was a strong movement called "regentrification," which simply meant that the upper classes of society, with some capital, were buying dilapidated Victorian buildings in downtown Philadelphia and were renovating them for their own use or to sell for large profits.

The primary purpose of the movement was to preserve and renew the architectural heritage of the big cities. The movement started in the late 1950s and was catching fire all over the country.

Pol read every book on real estate investing that he could buy or borrow. By the summer of 1980, they were ready to join the hundreds or thousands of renovators in Center City. (Parenthetically, Philadelphians were used to calling downtown as Center City.) Yeta and Pol were determined to succeed in their new venture. Their options were limited and they couldn't afford to fail!

Both of them were <u>eager to start a new career</u>, to learn new skills in a very different field. Everything was exciting! However, there was also fear of the unknown, of making mistakes!

After they got started, they kept on going! After a while, the tasks became easier and the outcome became more predicable: they would succeed in this new line of creativity because both were driven to survive and succeed!

Suddenly, they found themselves in <u>a life or death situation</u>! If they didn't generate a steady cash flow in two to three months, they could literally starve to death! The grave nature of their predicament made them <u>more focused, more dedicated and utterly determined to overcome every obstacle and to succeed spectacularly</u>!

Only time will tell! Their efforts during the first three or four months would be indicative of their success or failure!

Chapter Five.
The Investment Scheme

Yeta had a little bit of experience with renovation of dilapidated properties because her late husband, Sheldon, was a small Philadelphia developer. When Sheldon died in November 1978, he was in the process of renovating a court of ten "trinity houses." The popular example of a trinity house was the Betsy Ross House on 239 Arch St. in Philadelphia.

Betsy Ross House   Philadelphia

A trinity house was made up of three small boxes, stacked one on top of the other. The boxes were referred to, in the renovation trade, as Father, Son and Holy Ghost. Hence, the term "trinity house" came into use, which simply meant very small houses with three floors, connected by a narrow spiral staircase. The boxes were usually about ten by ten feet in diameter. They were built behind large houses owned by rich landlords during colonial times.

The trinities were hurriedly built houses, with only one course of bricks for walls, for the use of indentured servants. During colonial times, each floor housed a whole family, as many as eight or ten people. Each floor had a large fireplace, which the residents used to cook food and for heating the unit in winter. In the middle of the court yard was a primitive outhouse for the use of the whole community!

After Sheldon died, Yeta decided to finish the renovation of the court. She entered into a partnership with Stan Goderoff, a Center City developer. Goderoff obtained a construction loan from a commercial bank and rehabilitated all the ten buildings in less than six months. He listed the tiny houses for sale at $65,000 each with Plummer-Levitt Company.

Unfortunately, a new form of ownership, called *condominium (condo),* just arrived in town. Big developers from Chicago converted old hotels and apartment buildings into condos.

Yeta's trinity houses couldn't compete with the glamorous condos. A $65,000 could buy a large one bedroom condo, with a parking stall in Center City, the use of an Olympic size swimming pool in summer and an exclusive membership to a club house right in downtown Philadelphia.

Even at $60,000, the trinities still couldn't compete with the popular condos. To sell the units for less than $60,000 would mean selling at a loss!

The partners decided to dissolve the partnership in 1980 and declared bankruptcy. The lending bank foreclosed on the loan and took over the ownership of the houses.

It was this bankruptcy that cast a pall on what they were about to do: investing in real estate. Pol was concerned that the bankruptcy might have ruined Yeta's credit status!

****

In order to be more knowledgeable about real estate, Pol decided to obtain a sales license for the state of Pennsylvania. He attended an intensive one month-long seminar on real estate sales and took a licensing examination administered by the state. He passed it with flying colors!

He decided to work for the Plummer-Levitt Company, the largest in the business in Philadelphia. The real estate company employed over 50 salesmen. The employment would allow him access to the Multiple Listing Service, where all the real estate listings were published. Furthermore, he obtained a license to sell real estate so as to help sell Yeta's trinity houses. Unfortunately, his efforts didn't make any difference.

He wanted to work as a salesman for only a year. During the same period, he intended to study real estate investing. He wanted to concentrate on rental properties!

He wanted to study and compare all the financial figures: cash flow, expenses, taxes, depreciation, net income, property valuation and the fascinating concept called "leverage."

Leverage simply meant "using other people's money." Instead of paying cash for the whole purchase of a property, the buyer went to a lender, like a bank, and borrowed the money. This way, the buyer used only a little bit of his own money as a down payment. Then, he bought more properties by borrowing more money from any lender. The lender may be the seller or some private investors.

Incidentally, the concept of leverage, as an investment tool, hardly existed in the third-world countries because the concept of "credit" was very primitive and rarely used. Perhaps, the primary reason why credit was not openly extended to creditors was the lack of trust that the debtor may not pay the debt.

Pol's parents, for example, owned a convenience store (sari-sari), which extended short term credit to neighbors, friends and relatives, without any interest. However, long term credits, such as 30-year mortgages, were virtually non-existent. If you buy a $100,000 house in the Philippines, you must have that amount of money in cash. This was the common practice in ancient times.

Korean businessmen in Philadelphia, for example, were known to carry cash to the settlement tables. When they bought businesses in

Philadelphia, they arrived with suitcases full of cash. Since American businessmen were more used to receiving certified checks, they felt uncomfortable in dealing with green cash. They feared being robbed on their way to deposit the money in a bank.

Still, the Korean businessmen paid their purchases with greenbacks. If a purchase called for a million dollars to change hands, they arrived with several suitcases filled with cash! When they opened their suitcases, the Americans were flabbergasted!

****

Leverage is a form of <u>credit</u>, which is a relatively modern concept. The idea of leverage was borrowed from mechanics, which defined it as a "mechanical advantage or power gained by using a lever."

Hence, the investment system is called "leverage" because the borrowed money acted like a <u>lever</u>. In mechanical terms, a lever is a tool, like a crow bar or a bar of metal, used to lift or move heavier objects. In a similar way, a loan allowed the investor/buyer to control more expensive properties by using borrowed money as a lever.

Informally, the concept of leverage applies to any help one receives from others. For example, if you wanted to move a furniture, which is too heavy for you to carry, you leveraged your power by asking a neighbor or a friend to help you.

In fact, every tool, known to human beings, has been invented to leverage the human capacity to make things. Consequently, the general concept of leverage is as old as human beings. Even animals use tools to accomplish more difficult tasks. Just the other day, the author witnessed a crow drop a walnut on the street so the tires of cars might break it. The bird waited patiently as it perched on an electric wire. As soon as a tire broke the nut, the bird retrieved and ate it.

****

Because of the use of leverage in real estate investing, the return of investments is much higher than in other forms of investments where leverage is not used. For this reason, the author considers <u>leverage as the fortune cookies of investing.</u> It is the leverage that brings great fortunes to the investor!

For example, if you buy a house that costs $100,000 and you put down $10,000, you leveraged the purchase by $90,000. If you profited $5,000 from rental during the first year of ownership, the return of your investment was 50% of what you had actually invested. If you made another $5,000 the next year, the return of your investments in only two years was 100%. In two years, you had already recouped your principal. Thereafter, you use your tenant's rental payments to pay your mortgage. This is a perfectly legal and moral "highway robbery!"

Better still, if you buy properties with <u>seller financing</u> and <u>no money down</u>, you <u>leveraged the purchase 100%.</u> Normally, the financing provided by the seller is 80% of the cost and is the first mortgage. The seller may also grant a 20% second mortgage, with shorter duration.

Whatever profit the investor makes thereafter is found money! This was <u>the most ideal way of investing in real estate!</u> <u>This was the primary scheme Yeta and Pol would use in their investments: one hundred percent leveraged!</u>

****

The most common use of leverage, in our economy, is the use of a thin plastic called the "credit card." By extending financial credit even to consumers with marginal income, buyers are able to buy merchandise that they can't otherwise afford. By making the minimum payment, which is normally just the interest on the loan, poorer consumers are able to live on borrowed money. This is the simple meaning of leverage: borrowing money or using other people's money.

Unfortunately, there are people who are not able to manage debt and some resort to bankruptcy! For about seven years, the bankrupt consumer is forced again to use cash only. They are still able to participate in the economy but without any leverage.

Investment leverage in America dates back to colonial times. For example, going back to 1764, a British pamphleteer marveled that Americans spent "as much on the luxurious British imports as prudence will countenance, and often much more." The American Colonists bought expensive linens, tableware, watches, glasses, gloves, hats, furniture and much more, according to historian T.H. Breen of Northwestern University in his book, "The Marketplace of Revolution."

From 1740 to 1771, British exports to the colonies increased fivefold. The use of credit was common and some Philadelphia merchants "sold as much as 90 percent of their goods on credit."

Spending money, on credit, has become part of the American character. To make matters worse, personal savings has been going down even in recent years. In 1984, for example, personal savings was 10.8 percent of people's income. In 1995, savings went down to 4.6 percent. In 2004, it went further down to 1.8 percent. In June 2005, it hit zero percent. In August 2005, the Commerce Department reported that even people who have money in 401(k) and IRA contributions don't save any money because they borrowed against their savings!

This author is heavily in debt and loves the concept of debt! The US economy has been progressive and prosperous precisely because of the use of leverage!

Not long ago, US families gave parties to celebrate the paid off mortgage certificates of their houses. The celebration consisted in the burning of the mortgage certificates!

Whoever inspired this fad was misguided! In fact, they would be in a better financial position if the houses were refinanced and the owners borrowed more money and cashed in some of the equity that had accumulated over time. Then, the families would have a greater disposable income!

The US government purposely encourages the US citizens to go into debt especially in the purchase of their houses. For this reason, owners are allowed to deduct the real estate taxes and the interest they had paid for their mortgages from their taxable income! In other words, owning a house provides a good tax shelter for the home owners.

Today, there is a modern mortgage called reverse mortgage because a bank may send the borrower a check every month, instead of the borrower sending a check to the bank. The lender may extend to the borrower a large line of credit or give the borrower a cash amount at settlement.

The reverse mortgage system is based on the fact that a <u>house, over time, accumulates equity</u>. People who have owned their homes for a number of years have built up equity that may add up to several thousand dollars. Certain banks now allow senior citizens to withdraw some of the accumulated appreciation of their property to ease their financial burden by originating a reverse mortgage.

To qualify for this type of mortgage, you have to be at least 62 years-old. It is a wonderful instrument created especially for wise older borrowers. To get more information about reverse mortgages, call your bank. If your bank does not handle it, it should know which banks do it. The writer has a reverse mortgage on their primary residence in Florida for five years now and feels fortunate to have it. It provides them at least $2,000 income every month, for the rest of their lives.

****

Perhaps, the most sophisticated and profitable use of leverage is <u>trading in stock options</u>. Trading in stock options was first introduced to the Chicago Stock Exchange in 1973.

The reader should understand that options are not securities. They are called <u>derivatives</u> because they derive their value from the underlying stocks. The reason why buying or selling stock options has a high leverage is because <u>the investor pays only for the cost of the option</u> and yet the investor controls as much of the stock market as an investor who pays cash for his stocks. For every $1000 that an ordinary investor spends on the stock market, the <u>options trader spends only between $150 and $200 of his money</u>. Yet, the return of investment may be 500% or more.

Because options-trading is esoteric, very risky and has its own vocabulary, <u>the author will cover the subject very lightly and briefly</u>. His purpose of discussing the subject is just to expose the reader to <u>the secret approaches of leverage used by wealthy investors and by elite traders</u>.

The first important concept is what is called a <u>call option</u>. A call is the right to buy a specified amount of underlying securities at a specified price, on or before an expiration date. Every call option is a bundle of 100 shares. For example, an investor may buy a call for $60 per share. The expiration date may be in six months. The investor who buys a call option predicts that the value of the stocks will go up.

As the expiration date nears, the investor can easily calculate the value of the underlying stocks. If the stocks have gone up to $75 per share, the investor may decide to exercise his option and buy them. However, he does not have to buy the stocks. Instead, he may decide to sell his option for $75 per share. Other investors might predict that the appreciating stocks will continue to go up and buy his option.

It was also possible that his call option went down in value and would allow it to expire. What the investor lost was only the price of the option.

A <u>put option</u> is the right to sell a specified amount of the underlying securities at a specified price, on or before the expiration date. When an investor decides to buy a put option, he had predicted that the stock value would go down.

If you don't own the underlying stock, don't sell a put option because if the market goes against you, the potential risk is incalculable! For this reason, most trading houses prohibit the selling of <u>unprotected stocks</u> (stocks that you don't own).

<u>Straddle</u> is an option strategy which the investor uses when he believes a stock would move heavily but doesn't know whether the movement is up or down. He buys both a call option and a put option with the same price. If the stock goes up, his call option wins; if the stock goes down, his put option wins.

A <u>spread</u> is when the investor buys a call option and simultaneously sells another option with the same underlying securities. The computation of a spread is extremely complex.

Options trading can be very profitable if the investor knows what he is doing. The usual way of making money in the stock market is when the value of the stocks goes up. If the values go down, the investor could lose a lot of money.

As the reader now understands, one of the strengths of options trading is that <u>the investor may profit</u> <u>from both up or down markets</u> and limits his risks by buying or selling options, without buying any stocks. For example, a Florida trader claimed, "I made $12,000 in two months by using options."

Another trader from Arizona exhorted other traders, "Make money by using market volatility. I made $11,000 just on one trade." An Ohio trader said, "Control more assets for less money. I made a 100% return in three weeks."

****

While working for Plummer-Levitt Company, Pol was able to list and sell some properties, including some commercial buildings. The experience with Plummer-Levitt confirmed his initial hunch that money in real estate was not in sales but in leveraged investments. In all his readings and experience, he didn't come across agents who made millions from selling real estate, except a few agents who specialized in expensive properties in Palm Beach and Naples, Florida and Beverly Hills, California. All the real big money was in leveraged investments in first class locations.

When a Philadelphia real estate tycoon, Albert Greenfield, was asked what principles he followed in real estate investing, his answer was, "Location! Location! Location!" These three words and principles have become the classic cliché of real estate investing. Still, it will remain eternally true!

Knowing that they had virtually nothing as a start-up capital, they decided to focus on properties that only needed cosmetic renovation in first class neighborhoods. They would stay away from "shells" that needed major construction.

Cosmetic renovation meant carpentry repairs; replacing counter tops, sinks and cabinets; changing old appliances; laying new floor coverings; sanding hardwood floors; painting all the walls; pressure cleaning the stone or brick walls; landscaping the grounds and gardens and a curb appeal that was clean and upscale!

The **central principle** of their investment scheme was "seller financing," which ipso facto leveraged the purchase at least 80%. This meant that the seller would act as the lender and the buyers would service the loans by paying the mortgages directly to the seller.

The **second principle** was not to make any down payment simply because they had no money. This meant a <u>hundred percent leveraged purchase</u>. Part of the purchase negotiation was to ask the seller for a second mortgage of 20% of the purchase price so that the sale is "no money down."

After the sale of Yeta's home on 216 Delhi St., they could offer a small down payment, if the seller insisted on it. However, their investment capital was only $70,000, which was nothing compared to their ambition of controlling at least a million dollars worth of property.

Their **third principle** was to come across as <u>honest, trustworthy and responsible persons</u>. These moral traits were important because the sellers were not getting any money up front. Implicitly, the sellers had to <u>trust </u>that the buyers knew what they were doing, that they would renovate the properties and make them profitable so that they could make the necessary payments to the sellers.

In order to make the proper impressions on the sellers, they insisted on <u>meeting and negotiating with</u> <u>the sellers</u>. If real estate agents were involved, they instructed them to emphasize Yeta's American heritage, her career as a Public Broadcasting Station producer and Pol's long academic background.

<u>These principles are workable even today or any day</u>! For this reason, anyone at any age, can start a successful business in real estate anywhere in the world, but especially in America. However, this advice carries a caviat: "the investor must still have all his marbles for at least five years, at least while the investor is building his real estate empire!"

Pol had learned, for a while, that owners of houses with <u>no existing mortgages or low balance of mortgages</u> were receptive to offers of seller financing, with a good interest rate. For example, an eighty-year-old woman in Philadelphia was initially shocked when a young buyer made an offer of seller financing, which would balloon (become due in full) in ten years.

The elderly woman was in good health but was selling to be close to her daughter in Boston. When she saw that she would receive a monthly payment of $1,500 for ten years, she accepted the offer. She knew she would be financially independent for the next ten years.

After that, if she was still alive and healthy, she would be financially secure for the rest of her life.

The other properties that were good candidates for seller financing were <u>vacant homes owned by retirees and wealthy sellers</u>. Furthermore, houses that had been <u>on the market for more than sixty days</u> would be receptive to offers of seller financing. Seller financing could be beneficial to the seller because it could mean immediate sale, at a good price and at a decent interest rate.

The grim alternative is for the property to remain vacant and losing revenues. A vacant property is always a strong temptation to juvenile vandals!

However, the <u>best prospects for seller financing and no money down were the "fixer-uppers."</u> The owners of such properties were forced to take back the mortgage (seller financing) because the banks would not, normally, lend money on properties in that condition. These were the properties that Yeta and Pol were looking for!

By 1980, Yeta and Pol were ready to role up their sleeves and to start investing! They were suddenly *in season to begin a substantial business cash flow*!

Yeta and Pol in front of a Philadelphia Hotel called, "In Season"

Their first purchase, in August 1980, was a <u>five unit</u> <u>apartment building</u> on Catherine St. in south Philadelphia. The area was called "Bella Vista" (beautiful view) by the predominantly Italian-American residents. The property was only four blocks from Center City. Hence, potential tenants could walk to work or ride a trolley that passed through the area, just two blocks away.

Their <u>rental strategy</u> was to entice some Center City renters to reside further south for less money. Because of the good quality of the apartments, the tenants would be happy to reside in Bella Vista.

The Catherine St. apartment building was in a better condition than they were prepared to tackle. They jumped on the occasion to purchase the building because the new owner was running out of financial resources and he was having serious problems with one of his tenants. He accepted $65,000 for the property and financed the sale for seven years at ten percent. The seller accepted a small down payment of $3000 and granted a second mortgage of $7,000 at 10% for 5 years.

Four of the units had already been renovated and were already rented out when they closed the purchase. They inherited four tenants who, in their opinion, were paying below market rent. The new owners intended to raise the rents for the next tenants.

The fifth unit, which was a one bedroom apartment, needed complete renovation. They hired a "South Philly" contractor because the job was in South Philadelphia. (To Philadelphians, Philadelphia was affectionately called Philly; and South Philadelphia was South Philly).

The South Philadelphia area was predominantly ethnic. The region became extremely congested because of a social custom that prevailed in the area. When a son or daughter got married, the new couple tended to live close to the paternal or maternal home. It was also conceivable that the children wanted to live near their parents because the parents pressured them to do so.

Catherine St. Apartment Building

Neighborhoods in South Philly became closely-knit and some strange customs evolved. For example, many men went home to eat lunch, which their doting mothers had prepared for them. Since parking was very difficult to find, it was customary to park their cars in the middle of a one-lane street while they ate their meals. If an "outsider," who didn't know local customs, drove through the street and honked his horn to get through, the macho man would predictably yell at him or her in anger and utter some profanities! Thus, the aggressive behavior reinforced the odd and illegal custom!

The "natives," of course, knew the practice and tolerated it. When they saw a car or cars parked on the middle of the street, they just backed up and looked for another street to drive through. This strange custom had been around for several decades.

When Frank Rizzo, who was from South Philly, became mayor of Philadelphia in the 1970s, he allowed cars to be parked on the medians of streets. This practice was illegal even in South Philly but the police just looked the other way!

Everyone knew that there was such a thing as a "South Philly Way," which was tinged with the "Mafia Ways." Every outsider had to be very careful in South Philly!

****

The renovation of the fifth apartment took longer than they had expected. They had some problems with their contractor because he was unreliable. In fear and trembling, Pol dared to fire his first contractor! There was no problem because he admitted that he was negligent!

Fortunately, the second contractor turned out to be honest and dependable! The newly renovated apartment looked like new.

Yeta advertised the rental in the Center City daily. As she had predicted, the calls for rent came from the Center City. The first young woman, Ellen, who came to see it, rented it because the trolley trains were close by. She also found the neighborhood friendly, clean and picturesque! Many of the small townhouses had flower gardens in front.

****

The previous owner's problem tenant became even more serious. Their third floor tenant refused to show them the apartment. The whole floor was one large two-bedroom apartment, which they had never seen. For suspicious reasons, the male tenant refused to cooperate to show the unit during the negotiation phase of the purchase. They took the word of the agent that the apartment had been beautifully renovated. Since the agent had mentioned that the tenant had three cats, they suspected that the animals may have done some serious damage to the unit.

Their second floor tenant, Ellen, complained that she could smell something foul coming from the third floor. She also complained that every time she happened to pass by John, the third floor tenant, she felt nauseated because, as she put it, "He smelled like hell! I swear that the man has not taken a bath in six months!"

They called the tenant at home and at work and left messages. When he didn't return their calls, they sent him a registered letter stating that if he refused to allow them to inspect the apartment by a certain date, they would file eviction papers with the city.

As they had predicted, he vacated the premises just before the stated date, which was good. What was bad was that the cats had urinated and defecated right on the carpeting. The stench was so offensive and suffocating!

They had the carpeting and padding completely removed and had the hard wood floor sanded down. Still, the odor was very strong! Then, they sprayed the whole apartment with commercial grade chemicals. The chemicals had lessened the odor but they could still detect a slight residue! Perhaps, they should try to rent it to another tenant with cats. They were prepared to do that. Meanwhile, they were eager to test the rental market.

Yeta advertised the apartment, which was really charming. It had two fireplaces with ornate mantelshelves. The unit was spacious, with a thousand square feet of living space.

The first potential tenants arrived early at around eight in the morning. They were well dressed young men in their late twenties. As they were ascending the top steps to the third floor, one of them, Jerry, said, "Your previous tenants had cats in here."

"What makes you think there were cats in here?" Yeta asked.

"We're experts in odor control," the second man said, whose name was Jon. "We own a business that removes this type of odor from buildings."

Jerry added, "I'm sure you tried to remove the odor but didn't completely succeed. That is because the bacteria that caused the odor have gotten into the wood. You needed to inject the chemicals right into the wood."

Those observations alarmed the owners. It meant more expenses and work to make the apartment more rentable!

After they had inspected the whole apartment and had a chance to make a decision, Jerry, the senior partner said, "We will take the apartment and we will treat the odor free of charge."

The neophyte investors felt relieved and lucky! Then, Yeta introduced Ellen, their first tenant on the second floor, to Jerry. Within a year, Jerry and Ellen got married and Ellen moved up to the third floor. Jon, Jerry's roommate, moved down to the second floor. All the tenants were happy and getting along with each other!

****

Their next acquisition was to buy an <u>apartment building, which included a large two-floor-apartment that they could use</u> as their residence. They were living in a trinity house on 216 Delhi St., which was impossible to heat in winter. The walls were made of one course of bricks and had small holes in the walls that were at least a quarter inch wide. They could hear the winds howling and whistling through the holes in winter.

They glued plastic sheets on the walls to minimize the intrusion of cold air. Still, the baseboard heat couldn't properly heat the house.

Yeta had renovated the Delhi St. herself. She had <u>installed mirrors in the bathroom</u> on the second floor to make the small space appear larger. The only problem was that the <u>mirrors generated at least twenty reflections of the user</u>. It was a weird visual experience! Pol felt like there were 20 phantasms that happened to look like him that were all crowded in the same toilet! One workman simply refused to use it and went to a service station nearby to relieve himself.

She installed <u>sliding glass doors</u> on the first floor, which made it look modern. She planted flowers and ground covers in her garden behind the house. For privacy and protection, she installed a six-foot fence around the garden. Everyone called the house a "doll house." Every floor, including the basement, had a large fire place.

Pol listed the Delhi St. with Plummer-Levitt for $85,000. It sold, full price, in two days. The proceeds from the sale of this house, which was about $70,000, became their source of a small down payment. This small amount of money was their "seed money" or for lack of a better term, their <u>capital</u>.

Pol studied the Multiple Listing Service since he was looking for a suitable building for their residence. By word of mouth, however, Pol learned that there was a very unique building on 11th St. and

Pine St., just a block away from Delhi St. The building had <u>3 two-bedroom apartments</u>.

The first apartment was <u>a two-story unit on the first floor</u> and <u>basement</u>. The basement had been carefully renovated around 1920 as a <u>speakeasy</u>, (a hidden night club where liquor was served illegally to club members during prohibition years from 1920 to 1933. Members spoke softly or easily so as not to attract the police. Hence, the term "speakeasy" gained currency among the members.) It had a twenty-five foot wet bar, with several feet of copper plumbing to dispense beer and liquor. It had a twenty-five foot ornate brass railing for foot-rest. There were twenty fancy bar stools. The club could accommodate no more than 50 members.

Around the bar, hanging from the ceilings, were ornately designed fretworks and stained glass panels. In a hidden wall was a large vault for wine and liquor storage. Behind the house, on the ground level, was a large dome-shaped root cellar, where potatoes and other grains were stored.

The "Speakeasy" is the second row house from the right, with arched Palladian Windows on the first floor.

After the repeal of the prohibition in 1933, the basement was outfitted with a large kitchen that became part of the first floor apartment.

The unit had two bedrooms and a large living room, with a fireplace. Behind the building was a fifty-foot by one-hundred foot formal garden. It was one of the largest and the most beautiful formal gardens in the City.

<u>This unit became their own residence.</u> They rented out the second and third floors as two-bedroom luxury apartments. They rented out each apartment for $1,000 a month. The $2000 rent they received from the two apartments paid their mortgage for the whole building. They were, in fact, <u>living rent free</u> in a luxurious apartment. Life was definitely looking better!

The 25 foot wet bar for the "speakeasy"

The fretworks over the bar

Chapter Six.
An Encounter With The Mafia

One beautiful afternoon in early spring, 1981, one of their contractors, Bruno Pasiglia, brought up an interesting renovation project. He took Yeta and Pol to the Catholic Church in Villa Vista. Next to the Church was a massive and sturdy building that had been used as a nun's convent, then as a catechism school for children and for various other religious events in the village.

The Madonna House

For the past ten years, however, it had not been used for anything. The parish priest, Father Pietro Puglisi, wanted to sell it so he could change the roof of the Church.

Yeta and Pol talked to the priest to ascertain the prize and to inquire whether he was willing to finance the sale. They asked him permission to inspect the property, which he called the <u>Madonna House</u>. The property was truly awesome because the larger parts of the building were below the ground. The building offered various renovation possibilities.

Pasiglia suggested converting the large space into loft apartments, which would effectively use the entire space from the floor of a deep basement to the ceiling of the third floor. The floor would actually start at the large basketball court in the lower basement level. The basketball court measured about 50 feet wide, 100 feet long and about sixty feet high. Pasiglia estimated that about thirty modern, loft apartments could be carved out of the Madonna House. The asking price was only $300,000 and the Padre would finance the sale at 10% for ten years.

Pol roughly estimated that the loft apartments could rent at $1,000 a month. With 30 apartments, the monthly income would be $30,000. The yearly income would be $360,000 during the first year. The rents could be raised between 5%-10% every year, which was customary in Center City. The income of Madonna House alone could support their lifestyle because both of them were frugal.

The selling broker was a corpulent man, weighing at least 500 pounds, whom everyone called Fatso Italiano. Fatso was generally rumored as a mafia under boss. With his huge size, he could soon become the mafia boss of all bosses.

In spite of his mafia connections, Yeta and Pol impulsively made a $5,000 deposit for the purchase of the property. The priest accepted the offer and they started filing their application for a change of zoning. Of course, Pasiglia would be the contractor to do the big renovation.

Yeta asked her architect friend, David Beck, to draw the elevations of the proposed thirty loft apartments. David spent several days measuring the available spaces and a full two months to finish the drawings. Then, they scheduled a public presentation of the change of zoning at the church hall. The hall could comfortably accommodate about 100 people.

In fact, there were over a 1000 people milling around. Some people brought their own chairs and sat outside on the sidewalk. Yeta and Pol felt concerned that the crowd seemed to be emotionally charged! Some women appeared angry and hurled daggered looks at them! They had no idea why the crowd seemed agitated!

At exactly seven in the evening, the priest called the meeting to order. However, the crowd refused to be orderly! Immediately, Yeta and Pol recognized that the flock was an <u>angry mob</u>, who <u>protested not only the rezoning but especially the selling of the property for secular use.</u>

One elderly heavy-set woman said in a booming voice, "Turning this sacred house into apartments is sacrilegious! I learned my catechism there, my daughter and my grandchildren learned their catechism there. The church should use it only for religious purposes!"

Fr. Puglisi spoke to calm down the mob. "My dear parishioners, you know that the Madonna House has not been used for any function for several years now. The Church doesn't have the money even to maintain it. The roof of our Church is leaking because of storm damage. We need to raise at least $100,000 for a new roof. This was why I listed the Madonna House for sale."

A male middle-aged parishioner also spoke in anger, "Father, the parish will raise the $100,000 that you need for a new roof of our church. Just don't allow the heathens to live in the Madonna House, which is in the Church's holy grounds. I agree with Maria, who spoke earlier, that the secular use of the Madonna House would be sacrilegious, in my opinion!"

The priest spoke again. "We have a guest speaker who will explain to us what the new owners are planning to build within the Madonna House. I have personally looked at the plans and the development will be upscale and in good taste. When you see the artistic drawings done by Mr. David Beck, you will be proud to have that quality of development in our midst. Perhaps, if you listen to Mr. Beck, you might change your minds. He is the renowned architect in our city of brotherly love."

The angry crowd responded by yelling, in unison, "Booooooooooooooooooo! Booooooooooooo!" for about three minutes while they <u>pointed their thumbs down</u>! Mr. Beck didn't dare to say a word. He looked scared and feared that the crowd might attack him!

Padre Pietro asked for silence. "Silence!... Please!... Listen and allow Mr. Beck to make his presentation!"

A heavy-set middle-aged woman responded to the priest saying, "Why should I allow him to speak when I know I wouldn't agree with him?"

The crowd repeated and said in unison, "We wouldn't agree with him! We don't want him to speak!"

David Beck looked ashen; he feared for his life and safety! The priest, too, gave up! His parishioners had turned on him! Yeta and Pol were huddled in a corner of the room completely bewildered and fearful for their safety! They had no idea the hearing would turn against them!

****

The reason why the crowd could say phrases in unison was because they had already protested in the passed! The men and women who had spoken had been asked to say what they had said. The protest had been organized and the priest was aware of it! Unfortunately, he didn't share his knowledge with the buyers until later on.

Pol was suspicious that the protest was formally organized and explicitly asked the priest if there had been protests in the past. The Padre even admitted that there was a near riot when a developer called the parishioners "fanatics and superstitious!"

Yeta and Pol realized that they were in a bind! If they could not develop the property, then they should back out of the deal!

They went to their lawyer, Henry Davidson, to find out how they could legally get out of their contract.

Meanwhile, Yeta was experiencing nightmares and anxiety attacks! She feared that the fiasco could derail their new business venture. Pol, too, was anxious and concerned that the deal with Madonna House might end their desire to acquire more properties.

What both Yeta and Pol feared the most was that Fatso might refuse to void the sale! With that eventuality, they would be stock with a useless property and it could become a constant financial drain!

Mr. Davidson called a meeting of all the principals involved in his office on Broad St., in Center City. Before the meeting, he tried to find out everything about Fatso Italiano, the selling broker. What

Henry found out was that the initial deposit made by the buyers was not put in a separate escrow account as the law required. Fatso co-mingled it with his own money, which was illegal. Henry also confirmed that Fatso was a well-known Mafioso in South Philly and was a dangerous man to mess around with!

Nevertheless, during the meeting, which Henry moderated, he intimated that if the Madonna House deal was not voided, he would file a formal complaint with the State Real Estate Commission regarding the mishandling of the escrow money.

After hearing that information and the threat from Henry, Fatso quickly wrote a check for $5,000 for the buyers and declared the deal null and void! That was the end of a traumatic experience in South Philly! The experience cost them $20,000 for the architectural drawings, surveys, permitting fees and legal fees. Still, they felt liberated and "off the hook!"

They made sure that they learned the valuable lessons from the scary episode with the Madonna House. The first lesson was to stay away from South Philly and from any mafia influence! The second lesson was to look for a better neighborhood to buy properties to renovate, far away from South Philly. Fortunately, Philadelphia had several good neighborhoods. It was just a question of making a proper survey of possible investment areas. They would do their homework more carefully next time!

They also made a resolve not to listen to contractors who were just creating new jobs for themselves and their workmen. Thenceforth, they must initiate their own projects, but only after a thorough research of all the essential variables!

Chapter Seven.
The Big Coup!

Having narrowly escaped disaster in South Philly, they started looking for a better neighborhood, far from the influence and threat of the South Philly mafia. Using the Multiple Listing Service, Pol traced an elderly owner of at least fifty apartment buildings. They visited him in his office on Chester Ave. in what was called "University City" because it was around the University of Pennsylvania and Drexel University in West Philly.

Mr. Maxwell Schwartz, the real estate tycoon, should have stopped managing his properties five years earlier. Unpaid bills were piling all over his large disk and around the floor like small mountains. He had become too feeble to care for his many properties. Obviously, he wasn't paying his bills because the envelopes had not been opened. He dared his creditors to sue him or force him to act otherwise!

He was a perfect example of a seller who would be happy to finance the sales of his properties. He was actually begging Yeta and Pol to take over his crumbling real estate "empire!" And, being obviously rich, he didn't want any down payment. For whatever reason, he liked and trusted the buyers.

The prospective buyers put all their terms of ownership on the table before they even inspected any property, namely, seller financing for seven years at ten percent and no money down. Pol explained that they were asking him to grant to the buyers both a first and second mortgages.

Mr. Schwartz said, "Look at all the buildings I own and then make me offers. I'm flexible. I'll make it possible for you to acquire as many properties as you care to own."

They asked to see only his five best Victorian buildings! By then, the neophyte buyers knew exactly what they wanted to buy. Out of the five buildings, they intended to buy two or three if they liked what they saw!

His head repairman took them to see the buildings they had requested. In less than an hour, they had decided to buy three buildings. The two other buildings were in very bad condition.

While walking through the first floor of one building, water was cascading from the ceiling like a waterfall! Pol suspected that a water heater in the upper level had exploded and gallons of water were flowing from the tank! So much water was falling down from the second floor that they feared the ceiling might fall down over their heads!

They refused to see anything more of that property. What was unbelievable was the fact that there were tenants living in that waterlogged building. The other amazing thing was that the repair man was not alarmed by the cascading waters! It seemed that he was used to seeing greater catastrophes than what we were witnessing!

The first property they decided to purchase was <u>Ivy Hall</u> with <u>twelve apartments</u>. Ivy Hall was an elegant Victorian building, but it needed at least a cosmetic renovation. Yeta was certain that with a little TLC, it would shine like a precious stone!

Ivy Hall on 41st St. and Chester Ave. after the renovation

There were actually ten apartments in the front building and two more apartments in the rear building. The buildings were contiguous and, for all practical purposes, belonged to each other.

The front building was originally a luxurious estate, with eighteen-foot ceilings, fancy wood moldings and hardwood floors (white oak). The two rear apartments were plain and simple.

The reader should note that these large houses in University City were once <u>vacation homes of wealthy Philadelphians</u> in Victorian times. The ten units in the front building had been designed as large bedrooms. The plain building behind was obviously reserved for indentured servants, slaves and, if necessary, for extra guests.

It should also be noted that University City was no more than five or six miles from Center City. Still, that area was a good distance for the vacationers who traveled on horseback or slow-moving carts. They definitely hauled their cargoes using oxcarts.

After Philadelphia had naturally expanded to all directions, vacationing to West Philly no longer made sense. The character of the neighborhood had changed from country to urban. The wealthy Philadelphians sold or abandoned their vacation homes and bought vacation homes at the New Jersey shores, the Bahamas, the Caribbean Islands or somewhere else, which were more prestigious!

Because Ivy Hall was only a block away from the University of Penn campus, some investors in the 1950s converted the bedrooms into apartments by installing additional bathrooms and kitchens.

The same thing happened to the <u>two apartment buildings</u> on <u>Chester Ave.</u> Both buildings were also Victorian in architecture. Each building had five apartments. Those apartments were also large bedrooms in two separate buildings. They were later converted into apartments after they ceased to be vacation houses for the rich. The Chester Ave. buildings were only half a block away from Ivy Hall.

The Chester Ave. Buildings

They bought twenty-two beautiful apartments in one day, with seller financing and no down payment. They bought them because they were cheap! They bought Ivy Hall for $50,000 and the Chester Ave. buildings also for $50,000. However, they knew that after renovating them, they would rent at fair market value and those four buildings would be worth at least a million dollars.

Of course, they expected to encounter some problems in the process of making their first million! For example, when they made the settlement on Ivy Hall, Mr. Schwartz told the buyers that the oil tank was full of fuel. Yet, early the next morning, a tenant called that they had no heat. Pol went to check the fuel tank and found out that the tank was indeed empty.

He called for an oil delivery service. He had to pay cash the first time, until he had established his own account with the oil supplier. He paid $450 for the delivery and expected the fuel to last for several days or weeks. Yet, the next day, the tank was empty again!

Pol started to feel panicky and wondered whether they had made a mistake in buying old buildings! He was thinking that if the heater burned up that much fuel every day, there was no way they could make money in rental properties!

Pol made an appointment with a heating specialist. The specialist discovered that the firing chamber of the heater was too large for the heater. It was the same firing chamber that was used when the owners used steam for heating.

The specialist suggested building a much smaller brick chamber, approximately one tenth of the existing one. Then, he installed a new thermostat, which could be programmed, in one of the smaller apartments on the first floor and locked it. Only Pol could program or reprogram the mechanism. The thermostat could be programmed to stop heating after the tenants had left the building for work and to restart it when the tenants returned home.

Those adjustments made a lot of difference. Suddenly, a full tank lasted for at least a month. <u>Pol exhaled like a banshee</u> after he realized that money could be made from dilapidated properties! Their investing scheme seemed to be right on target!

The reason why a full tank was used up every day was due to the fact that the old thermostat had been installed in the first floor hallway. Every tenant had access to the control box. Every tenant foolishly set the thermostat at the highest setting in order to generate maximum heat!

Of course, every apartment became overheated! Pol found out that the tenants controlled the heat in their apartments by opening all the windows and, at times, also their doors, which made them vulnerable to robbery or burglary!

In effect, the buildings were heating the whole neighborhood! Pol learned later on that opening windows to control the temperature of an old apartment was a common practice everywhere in the city especially in buildings with antiquated heating systems.

The closing of the sale for Chester Ave. apartments was delayed a couple of weeks because of <u>a serious violation of an important stipulation in the sales contract.</u> The contract explicitly stated that the leases of the existing ten tenants would be assigned to the new owners and the rent money would be prorated at settlement.

Without informing the buyers, Mr. Schwartz evicted all the tenants and left the properties completely empty! By evicting the tenants, he didn't have to repair the temperamental heaters!

The buyers went to their lawyer, Henry Davidson, and asked his legal advice. "My advice is for you to <u>assess monetary</u> compensation for lost revenues. Leave the wording of the document to me."

The next day, Henry called and read the document he had composed. It read,

"Dear Mr. Schwartz,

"As the lawyer for the Mabulbuls, I'm informing you that the buyers will assess monetary damages from you for evicting the ten tenants from the Chester Ave Apartments without their consent. They had intended to keep those tenants for six months, while they were renovating Ivy Hall. I have estimated that the financial damage would be for the whole six months. The monthly loss of income for the buyers would come to $700 per month and the total loss for six months would come to $4,200 per unit. Since there are ten apartments, the total loses would come to $42,000.

"As their lawyer, I'm assessing you $20,000 punitive penalty for violating my client's rights. Please bring a check for $62,000 at settlement. I'm giving you two days to accept or reject this proposal. If you reject it, my clients will file a formal suit and demand higher compensation.

Sincerely, Henry Davidson."

Within hours, Schwartz called Henry that he was accepting his proposal. This new development, which allowed the buyers to <u>walk away from the settlement table with</u> <u>additional cash,</u> led them to the <u>fourth investment scheme</u> by the real estate investors. The new scheme was <u>to look for legal transgressions</u> by the seller and <u>walk away from settlement with additional cash!</u>

This transaction was too good to be true. They purchased twenty two apartments without using one penny of their money. On top of 100% leverage, they received $62,000 from the seller. Pol wondered how often they could use this fantastic scheme! He made a <u>resolve to be vigilant of similar situations because he felt certain that other sellers would also try to defraud them!</u>

****

The Chester Ave. apartment buildings were also having serious heating problems. The heating system was a "one pipe steam mechanism." This meant that the steam rose to the second and third floor radiators. But, after the steam had cooled off and became liquid again, it flowed back to the heater by using the same pipe used by the steam. The collision between the steam and cold water produced loud banging noises!

The crowding of the two elements in one pipe made the system less efficient and the third floor radiators were not getting enough heat. The heating specialist suggested that the heating system be completely replaced!

It made sense but they couldn't afford the replacement because, by then, they were completely broke! Their small capital of $70,000 was completely gone! The $62,000 found money was needed to continue renovating the apartments. By that time, they had already accepted tenants and they were committed to finish at least ten apartments within a month.

Pol decided he would study everything there was to learn about the steam heating system. He read all the literature and attended seminars. He talked to every specialist at the heating conferences and seminars.

He finally understood the proper techniques for balancing the flow of the steam heat so that it could reach especially the third floor radiators. The <u>secret was in using a key</u> to bleed the radiators at the beginning of every heating season. By bleeding all the radiators especially in the third floor the radiators became more efficient and balanced. His efforts to solve the heating problems of Chester Ave. apartments saved them thousands of dollars.

Meanwhile, they learned how to <u>obtain cheap money from commercial banks</u> to use for renovation. There was a government program precisely designed to rehabilitate dilapidated properties. It was called <u>Title One, which was administered by HUD</u> (Housing and Urban Development).

They went to a commercial bank and applied for it. The <u>construction loan was guaranteed by the government in order to encourage greater housing development</u>. Hence, the bank lent the money at a very low interest rate, approximately two percent. This new source of capital allowed them to renovate all the twenty-two units in three months.

Every unit got rented before they were actually finished. Yeta and Pol had developed <u>an artistic and imaginative approach</u> <u>to renovation</u> so that the potential tenants were excited to live in their buildings. Very often the applicant would say, "I'll take it" before he or she had looked at the rest of the apartment. This often happened when the apartment had <u>a loft or an attic for sleeping quarters.</u>

They were getting calls from potential tenants asking for loft apartments. Those requests confirmed their hunch that loft apartments were hot especially with younger tenants! They decided to look for more buildings that had high ceilings, which they could convert to loft apartments. The property below would have been suited for more innovative renovation.

A Gothic Revival in University City, Philadelphia

Chapter Eight.
Common Traits of Successful Investors

It goes without saying that not everyone will succeed in real estate investing. If you dread or fear dealing with tenants and their problems, you're not suited to manage properties and tenants. If you don't know or don't want to make repairs to properties, leave the management to others.

Pol's background was highly academic. Yet, he realized, early on, that if he was going to own and manage rental real estate, he had to learn how to make repairs because he found out that trades men didn't want to do <u>small jobs</u>. Yet, most of the needed repairs were very small and may take only a couple of minutes to do. For example, leaky faucets, burnt out bulbs in hallways and corridors, broken window glasses and sticky locks were small jobs. Still, they needed immediate attention.

Leaky faucets, for example, could cost the landlord high water bills. Moreover, tenants with leaking faucets complain about the annoying noises that disturb their sleep. The repair consists in changing the washer, which takes no more than two minutes. Burnt out bulbs could cause accidents and high liability insurance, not to mention law suits. Changing burnt bulbs consists in getting a ladder and removing the burn out bulb and changing it with a new one. This repair would take no more than two minutes.

Locks that were stuck could make living in an apartment unsafe and make the landlord liable to further law suits. Locks that malfunction might just need a squirt of oil, which takes only seconds to do. Or, it might need a replacement, which might take five minutes to do.

Workmen could be very choosy because there were not enough good workers and the demand for reliable workers was excessive! The whole city of Philadelphia was being renovated! Consequently, tradesmen could afford to limit their work only on jobs that lasted for several hours, several days or even weeks.

Fortunately, there was a <u>special category of workers</u> who were called <u>handymen</u>. They were clever and skillful workmen who could do different types of repairs, from carpentry to plumbing and electricity and so on. Due to their versatility, they charged much more money for their labor. In some cases, they charged ten times more than the regular workmen. Still, handymen were a blessing especially to older men, helpless widows and unskilled landlords to do small jobs.

There was one important reason why landlords needed to know how to do quick repairs to rental properties. In big cities like Philadelphia or New York, there were criminal elements, who broke into apartment buildings by kicking the front doors, kicking the apartment doors, walked in and trashed the apartments for the prospect of finding cash, jewelry and other valuables! When crimes of this kind occur, the landlord should be able to do the necessary repairs to the main door, to all the apartment doors that had been damaged; change all the locks and secure the premises from potential new burglaries and robberies.

In June 1983, for example, Yeta and Pol were victimized by a burglar to the ten apartments on Chester Ave. In a brief period of about ten or fifteen minutes, a burglar had kicked in the main door and kicked every door of the ten apartments. The burglar had a "big foot;" he left 15 inches long footprints on every door!

For three solid hours, Pol repaired all the damages. By the time the tenants arrived from work or from classrooms, Pol had already repaired the damages. He left a notice at the front doors of each building to see him in his office. He was waiting to give each tenant his or her new keys and to explain what had happened. He saved money on the repairs and made his tenants feel safer and comfortable in living in his properties.

****

What does a good real estate investor need to possess? Pol asked this question from about 500 people of different ages, professions in Philadelphia as part of his research for this chapter.

<u>Being a good handyman</u> would definitely help a lot. Most people whom the author had interviewed tended to think that what he or

she needed was sufficient money to start a real estate business. Pol's findings may surprise the reader; money is not necessary! Good credit and reputation are more important than money. Money only gives the more affluent investor a head start. However, if he is not smart and realistic, he may lose all his money with his first transactions!

A smart investor will study and learn whatever *knowledge* is necessary to make sound investment decisions.

However, there has to be a limit to any knowledge acquisition. You can never know enough about a subject matter before you have to make important decisions. Very often, you decide based on partial knowledge, intuition, mere hunch, instinct and shear luck! It goes without saying that you will make some mistakes.

If you make a mistake, as you certainly will, learn from it! Remember that to err is human! Just don't keep on making the same mistakes!

The next important trait is a realistic vision of what to expect. You have to look at the whole picture: both positive and negative and everything in between. Remember that a coin has more than two face: heads and tails and a sizable edges. Assuming that you are dealing with "fixer-uppers," before owning a property, have a realistic estimate as to how much it would cost to renovate it and where the necessary funds would come from. How long would the renovation take? How much rent can you realistically expect from each unit?

To have a good idea of a fair market rent, you have to invest some time in checking out what your competitors are asking for the same or similar apartments. Ask a lot of pertinent questions.

There is a generally accepted rough estimate of what an apartment or a house could rent for. A housing unit should be able to rent for at least one percent of its value per month. Using this principle, an apartment that is valued at $70,000 should rent for at least $700 per month. Of course, some cities are more expensive than others and charge much more because, in some cities, the demand for housing far exceeds the supply. What the landlords actually get for rent is based on the economic principle known as supply and demand equation.

If the demand is higher than the supply, it is called a <u>landlord's market.</u> This means that landlords can charge more money than expected. However, if the supply exceeds the demand, it's a <u>renter's market</u>. This means that potential tenants can bargain for lower rent or demand more amenities.

Places like Los Angeles rents, on average, 3.3% of the value of the property per month. New York City, on average, rents apartments at 4.3% of the value and San Francisco rents, on average, at 4.5% of the real estate value.

In contrast, Philadelphia rents, on average, at only 1.8% of the value. Atlanta rents only at 2.0% of the real estate value; while Denver and Houston rent at 2.2% of the value. Of course, these percentages will change depending on the supply and demand equation.

The next important trait is a <u>good imagination</u>, which can improve the curb appeal of your properties. Curb appeal is important, if you want to <u>attract good quality tenants</u>. Good quality tenants will maintain the curb appeal of the property by picking up the trash and liter from the premises. Good tenants will project the beautiful appearance and prosperity of the property by the way they dress and carry themselves. Because they are proud of their residence, they will help you maintain the condition of the apartments and keep their appliances and furniture clean and attractive.

Good imagination will help your choice of colors both inside and outside the buildings. Imagination will help you improve the <u>landscaping</u>, which also <u>enhances the curb appeal of the apartment or house</u>.

The next useful traits are <u>critical thinking skills</u>. You need to be analytic and critical about your own thinking and the thinking of those who work with you. Critical thinking clarifies your vision of what you need to do to improve your properties. For example, some of the apartments Yeta and Pol owned had high eighteen-foot ceilings. Critical thinking led them to add <u>lofts</u> for sleeping areas, which increased the square footage of the apartments. It also added novelty and drama to the units.

In the third floors, they <u>opened up the ceilings</u> and built stairs and turned the attics into additional sleeping quarters. These innovations appealed to younger and more affluent tenants because they were different and imaginative.

Your other useful trait is <u>people skills</u>. Robert Allen, who wrote the best selling book "No Money Down," claims that "real estate is a people business." This is especially true if you manage rental properties. You can never know enough about the potential tenants. You must know enough about human nature, human psychology and have a good common sense to identify liars and bad elements. <u>Choosing good tenants</u> is essential to your success as an investor. A bad tenant can wreck your property in hours or just days. And, evicting a bad tenant may take months of aggravation! Meanwhile, you're losing money because you're not getting the rent as you should!

Another important trait is <u>good communication skills</u>. You have to communicate properly as you negotiate a sale or purchase of a property. You have to communicate well with every tradesman working for you and avoid misunderstandings. You have to communicate well with the tenants as you explain that they have to pay their rent on time, what the penalties are for late payments. You have to explain clearly that they have to open their own accounts for electricity, water and gas. You have to explain clearly that they have to mow the lawn if they rent houses and so on.

One other important skill is how to <u>negotiate fairly</u> in the sale or purchase of real estate property. A fair negotiation is a "win-win" situation in which each negotiator feels that he won something in the process. Allow the other party to save face and to feel like a winner! Learn the valid and fair techniques of negotiation so that you use immediate responses or intentional delays to send a clear message without words.

<u>Be truthful, generous and considerate to good tenants</u> who have a hard time paying the fair rent. Providing decent housing is a public service; but owning rental properties is primarily an investment. Still, there should be some kind of compromise and consideration for changing situations.

There is a common practice among service trades called <u>cost shifting.</u> What it means is that they charge more from those who can pay and less from those who have less. Yeta and Pol are among the practitioners of cost shifting. For some of their tenants, they raised rents in very small increments. Some of their tenants have been their, de facto, <u>charities</u>. Some of their tenants have rented from them for more than fifteen years. Some are on fixed income and are renting at below market value.

The cost shifting is really with the new tenants who have more resources. The new tenant doesn't know that he is paying much more than the other tenants. In a similar way, the old tenant doesn't know he is paying below market value. Just make sure that the low rent still covers the mortgage amount.

Have a <u>good sense of humor</u>! It allows you to get through crisis, accidents and unforeseen untoward events! It allows you to maintain good health. Laughter has been known as a good medicine; humor too belongs to the same medical and psychological prescription.

Finally, as already mentioned in the beginning, be prepared to <u>learn as many trades for repairing small jobs as necessary</u>. The shortage of good workers has created great frustration among landlords. Pol had been stood up by many workers who never showed up for small jobs. Learn all the skills necessary to maintain the physical safety especially of <u>female tenants</u>. Learn especially how to fix or replace locks. If the lock of an apartment had been compromised, change it as soon as possible and repair the other damages in the apartment.

The special reward of "knowing how to repair things" is the realization that you can do more than you had ever imagined! This realization will raise your self-esteem a few notches upwards. It is a <u>good feeling to know that you can do almost anything that you decide to do</u>!

This feeling of confidence and higher self-esteem may motivate you to do art, without any training. This was what happened to Pol: he became an artist. He became a sculptor, a painter, an artistic gardener, a maker of mosaics and collages and other media. See chapters twelve and sixteen of this book.

In his book, *Everyone Is An Artist: Making Yourself the Artwork*, (IUniverse, 2003) the author argued that artistry is innate. The only thing an art student can learn from teachers is methodology. Teachers can teach little tricks of creating certain effects. But the artistry that is necessary for the formation of artistic concepts is inborn!

Chapter Nine.
Dividing Responsibilities

From the first day of their marriage, Yeta took care of their finances. She kept all the money and the record books. It worked that way in Pol's own family in the Philippines and he himself felt comfortable about it. Yeta was equally happy with that role because she felt more financially secure.

It seemed natural for Pol to deal with the workmen who were all males. He also handled the origination of loans and took over the negotiation of the sale or purchase of properties.

Still, there were gray areas where neither one of them was certain about the responsibilities. One day, they had a mild but unpleasant argument about the color to paint the outside of a building. From Pol's point of view, the color didn't matter. The buildings were only rental properties and one color was as good as another. Yeta, on the other hand, had a degree in interior design and coordinating colors was important to her.

To minimize the friction and arguments, Pol proposed that Yeta take charge of everything inside the buildings and the color of the exterior walls. She was also in charge of the tenants. This specific responsibility alone outweighed all the others because it was an ongoing and sometimes terribly aggravating burden!

The aggravation levels depended on the number of units involved and the quality of the tenants. One tenant alone who felt unhappy could cause so much tension and aggravation! For instance, one tenant by the name of Richard traded his carpentry skills for his rent. For four months, he didn't do any work and was not paying any rent. They decided to evict him and the case was tried in court. He lost the case and was legally evicted!

The legal aspects of the case were simple and clear. The psychological and moral aspects, however, were more complex. As soon as they served him the eviction notice, Richard decided to break them down by leaving one hour messages on their voice machine several times a day! He was arguing his case and making excuses why he didn't do his job. Talking to him over the phone was impossible because he couldn't listen to reason.

Richard was, in fact, a schizophrenic person. He had been committed to an insane asylum by his own parents. A tenant like Richard could easily drive a landlord crazy!

Accepting Richard as their tenant was partly Yeta's fault. She rented to him for the wrong reason: because she knew Richard's mother. They had been members of the "Philadelphia Fellowship House," founded by Quakers for the promotion of racial equality and harmony. This acquaintance with the mother led her to assume, wrongly, that Richard would be a good tenant. If she had investigated his background, she would have found out that the man was mentally ill.

Probably, the most difficult responsibility for Yeta was choosing the tenants and dealing with their problems. Some of their tenants were college students from affluent homes. They didn't know how to defrost refrigerators and often forgot their keys. The case of Richard illustrated how difficult her responsibilities could be. Her six months ordeal with Richard would eventually burn her out!

And, Pol's most important responsibilities were making repairs and maintaining all the properties. When dealing with ancient buildings, repairs could be mysterious and really difficult because he had to know and understand the old technologies and materials used in the original construction. All of the properties were over one hundred years old. For example, old plumbing used lead that caused lead poisoning. He had to remove and change all the lead plumbing wherever he found them.

One of his problems with old buildings was the use of laths and plaster, which was the old technique of framing walls. The modern method used wallboards and wet spackle, made out of powdered gypsum. Still, it was necessary to remove the old plaster and laths in order to construct clean and smooth walls. Removing laths was always a heavy physical work!

The gardening and landscaping were joint decisions. These were the more enjoyable projects because they came under the category of "finishing touches." When they were at the gardening phase, they knew that they were almost done with the property! They could already see the light at the end of the tunnel.

Each one had the privilege of consulting with the other at any time. Since they worked at the same location, they could consult with each other very often. <u>This on-going consultation cemented their marriage!</u>

The division of responsibilities worked like magic! Even though they worked together every day, each one stayed within his or her sphere of responsibilities.

Since they still manage some rental properties today, the same division of labor still holds. In over twenty-five years of working together, they never fought or argued again about anything that has caused serious dissension between them!

****

Using the *Title One* money, which they borrowed from Germantown commercial banks, they methodically renovated all the twenty-two apartments that they had purchased from Mr. Schwartz.

At first, they had problems with the workmen who were actually lying to them and cheating them about their wages. Their painter, Mart Wagner, who was the husband of Yeta's friend, Patricia, had convinced them that they should pay the workers <u>time and materials</u>. This meant that at the end of the week, the workers totaled the number of hours they had worked and were reimbursed for any materials that they had purchased during the week.

Pol had wrongly assumed that workmen were basically honest. Except for Mart, he quickly suspected that the workers were lying about the number of hours they had worked. For example, everyone claimed that they started working at seven in the morning.

One day, Pol woke up early and was at the job site by seven. Mart arrived at 10 o'clock. The next worker arrived for work just before eleven. Pol and Yeta habitually arrived at the job site just after eleven. By arriving just before eleven, the worker could then claim to have worked since seven or six. They assumed that Pol would never know the truth. They misjudged him!

He immediately fired all his cheating workmen! Thenceforth, he asked three contractors to bid on every job. He chose the ones who impressed him for whatever reason. If none of the contractors impressed him, he interviewed more contractors until he felt satisfied.

After a while, <u>the good</u> <u>and the honest contractors stood out</u> and he rewarded <u>them with new contracts</u>!

Renovating apartments became easier after Pol and Yeta had <u>formulated a certain routine</u>. First, they vacated the whole building of tenants. Vacating a building was easy because the tenants had already expected to move out. Still, Yeta promised the departing tenants that she would rent to them again after the renovation was finished. She knew also that she was just trying to be polite. After the renovation, they wouldn't be able to afford the higher rent.

Then, they removed all the old appliances, changed the floor covers or sanded the hardwood floors, repaired all the damage to the walls and woodwork, painted all the walls and woodwork, installed new appliances and kitchen cabinets, pressure cleaned the stonework and brick walls, redesigned the gardens and planted ground covers and specimen plants.

In three months, they finished and rented out all the twenty-two apartments. In a short time, they had <u>increased the values of each property</u> at least ten fold. The rents were competitive and fair.

****

They bought another <u>ten-unit apartment building</u> in South Philly, near their first purchase on Catherine St. They went back to South Philly because Rosa Paglia, whom they had met in Bella Vista, had a nephew who was selling four apartment buildings. She owned some apartment buildings herself.

Her nephew, Pietro, from Sicily had inherited four buildings from her brother who had died just a few months earlier. Rosa was certain that Yeta and Pol would be interested in at least one of the buildings. The building had a reddish brick walls and was only two blocks from the famous <u>Italian market</u> where everything was cheaper than in any grocery stores. The Italian market was a positive amenity for many tenants because of the freshness of their fruits and vegetables! One can buy almost anything in the Italian market!

The apartments had already been renovated but in poor quality. Yeta and Pol wanted to impose their own standards and renovate the apartments again in order to rent to better quality tenants. They had to change all the appliances, the kitchen cabinets and the floor coverings. They also had to repaint the whole building.

When they bought the building, all the tenants were refugees from Cambodia and Vietnam. The refugees from Cambodia were, *Hmongs*, who had been nomads in the Cambodian forests. There was a rumor among the neighbors that the *Hmongs* hunted pigeons in the town squares and were suspected of stealing people's pet dogs and cats for food. Pol couldn't easily dismiss the rumors because, in the old country, the *Hmongs* ate anything they could kill or find. They were nomads and survived in whatever way they could.

The Vietnamese too had some strange customs that disgusted some Americans. For example, on weekends, they had many visitors who were also refugees. They would eat fried chicken, from MacDonald, on the front porch and threw the bones and unwanted parts on the sidewalk. To them, there was nothing unsanitary about the behavior because, back in the old country, stray dogs would happily eat the bones and other left over thrown to them. The only problem was that there were no stray dogs or cats in South Philly. The chicken bones and other left over parts only attracted swarms of flies!

The tenth St. apartments

One day, a Hmong woman was chasing a live chicken on the stairway of the building. The fowl had escaped from her apartment. An American male tenant was on his way to work and tried to help her catch the fowl. As he was about to catch the hen, the woman hit him on the head with a bamboo cane to prevent him from catching the animal. She mistakenly thought that the American was trying to steal her chicken.

They evicted all the refugees in order to upgrade the apartments. By upgrading the apartments, they would also up-graded their tenants.

Their intended clientele were not refugees, but young professionals who worked in Center City.

Finally, they bought two more Victorian apartment buildings on Cedar Avenue, at the University City in West Philly. Each building had five units. Those were Victorian beauties with stained glass windows. Some of the stained glass windows contained balloon motifs that celebrated the 1876 World Exposition held in the famous Fairmount Park in Philadelphia.

The Cedar Ave Apartments

Pol wanted to experiment if they could walk away with some cash at the settlement as they had done in the settlement of Chester Ave. Both Yeta and Pol were quite certain that the Cedar Ave properties might be their last investment ventures.

They visited their lawyer, Henry Davidson, and asked him to enclose in the purchase offer the following clause, "The seller agrees to evict the existing tenants by the time the sale is closed on June 1, 1983." This clause, if complied with, would expedite the renovation of the two buildings. Pol could get his crew ready to work right after the closing of the sale. Pol was also looking for any infraction, which he could justify an assessment of some cash at settlement!

Sure enough, the ten tenants of Cedar Ave had not been evicted. The seller completely forgot the existence of the <u>eviction clause</u>. At settlement, Henry was kind and gentle to the seller and assessed him only $35,000. Still, walking away with extra cash at settlement maybe more common than he had imagined!

****

Yeta and Pol had recently visited San Francisco, only months earlier. They admired the multi-colored Victorian houses called, "Painted Ladies." Since the two Victorian buildings would likely be their last acquisitions, Yeta decided to indulge her fantasy of creating two painted ladies in Philadelphia. She selected twelve different colors to decorate her buildings. They were spectacular!

Renting all the ten apartments was easy because most of the apartments either had lofts or had sleeping quarters in the attics. Those were the apartments coveted by the University of Pennsylvania students.

They could finally relax and enjoy what they had accomplished in less than four years. Their investment scheme worked as they had planned it. Pol was planning to go on a long cruise to the Caribbean Islands. Yeta, on the other hand, was thinking of retiring to Florida.

How would they solve this big differences between them? Was Yeta going to leave Pol?

Chapter Ten.
Tenancy Problems

In the previous chapter, the author had mentioned Yeta's on-going problems with the mentally ill tenant called Richard. The tenant was so demented that he tried to kill her! One late afternoon, Pol just happened to notice Richard carrying a machete, without a scabbard, as he walked towards their basement office on Chester Ave. Pol knew that Yeta was in the office, paying some bills. He instinctively suspected that Richard had evil intentions!

He found a two by four piece of lumber and picked it up as a weapon! He ran right into the office! Richard was already inside and was about to whack Yeta with his machete! Just in time, Pol struck the madman on the head and disabled him! Then, he called the police department who took Richard to the Pennsylvania mental hospital. To make sure that he was no longer a threat to their safety, they sued him for attempted murder!

When he became conscious, the policeman guarding him, arrested him and locked him up in prison. He stayed in prison for three months until his parents won a court order to transfer him to a mental hospital!

****

Selecting a tenant to fill a vacancy was very risky because the landlord knew very little about the applicant. There was always a possibility that the applicant was lying and intended to take advantage of the owner. Even after Yeta had verified the references, it was still possible that the personal references were not previous landlords but friends, family members or even partners in crime!

Based on their long experience with rental properties (over 25 years), Yeta and Pol learned that they were especially vulnerable when an apartment or a house had stayed vacant for more than sixty days. Normally, a vacant unit was rented within a week after it was advertised. For example, they had a vacancy in Cape Coral, Florida, during the Christmas season of 1991. The rental was actually being handled by Home Hunters, a management company that had handled their leasing contracts for over fifteen years.

In January 1992, Yeta placed an advertisement in the local paper to get some idea of the rental market. The US economy was going through a recession and Yeta was feeling unhappy and nervous with the prolonged vacancy!

To her surprise, she was deluged with phone calls. However, when she checked out the applicants' credit history, she found out that everyone had serious financial problems, like bankruptcy, large debts and very low credit ratings!

According to Darlene Simons of Home Hunters, who handled rentals for them, the same names kept appearing every time there was a new advertisement of properties for rent. They kept applying for residence because no professional managers would rent to them. Occasionally, a new landlord would enter the rental market. Lacking the necessary experience and knowledge, he or she would likely rent to one of those losers!

When a landlord mistakenly puts a bad tenant in his house or apartment, the <u>tenant would pay only the first month's</u> rent and a <u>fraction of the security deposit</u> in order to received the keys and occupy the unit or house. The new tenant would predictably make all kinds of promises to pay the rest of the security deposit in a week or two.

<u>The next month, the tenant would likely fail to pay his rent because he really can't afford it.</u> If the landlord gets angry and threatens to evict the deadbeat, the tenant may retaliate and may destroy the property in a short period of time. As a group, deadbeat tenants harbor deep-seated anger against landlords whom they assume to be filthy rich and heartless!

One time, Yeta rented a house in Florida to a woman in her late thirties with two teenage sons. The boys became involved with drugs and used the house for drug transactions. Strange vicious men were continually going through the house. The woman couldn't control her sons and the neighbors became afraid of the bad influence of the drug dealers on their own children. Drug users and the drug culture brought down property values!

Neighbors immediately informed Yeta about the drug dealing. She promptly evicted the tenants. Unfortunately, it took her three months to get them out of the house. By that time, they had virtually destroyed the house! It cost her more than $12,000 to put the house back in rental condition.

Five years earlier, Yeta rented a house to a family "because they had cute kids." The rental house was situated next to the house owned by Charles Ferrante, a Lee County Sheriff. Yeta called two of their references who gave her glowing testimonials about the whole family. Yeta felt convinced that she had the ideal tenants.

About four months later, Sheriff Ferrante called her and told her that his new neighbor was a convicted criminal and that he had personally arrested the man in a burglary.

Before she could evict the tenants, the ex-convict was arrested by his own employer, Hess Company. He was steeling cash and all kinds of merchandise from the company. When the police searched his rented house, the garage was full of stolen goods. He landed in jail for four years and the rest of his family had to move in with relatives in Ohio.

Of course, their worst experience was with the madman, Richard. However, they had other bad tenants in Philadelphia. For instance, Yeta accepted a couple for the first floor apartment on Chester Ave. For three months, the woman was never seen outside the apartment. Then, suddenly, the other tenants smelled foul odor coming from their apartment.

Pol tried to enter the apartment to find out what was causing the odor but they refused to cooperate. The odor was progressively getting worse and the tenants of the nine other apartments were threatening to move out. Pol felt pressured to do something drastic! He asked all the other tenants to inform him as soon as the suspicious tenants left their apartment for whatever reason!

When the tenants left the apartment for a doctor's appointment, Pol quickly changed the locks and locked them out! He waited for a phone call to negotiate the situation. He was prepared to go to court or even to go to jail, if necessary!

After a week, the husband called to inquire about their cat but said nothing about removing their belongings from the apartment.

After another week, Pol hired workers to remove their things and stored them in the basement. The workmen cleaned the apartment and prepared it for rental. What the workmen found that caused the smell were at least twenty large buckets of urine. It looked like the couple was involved in a strange <u>urine fetish!</u>

One of the other tenants on Chester Ave., who had some contact with the odd couple, mentioned to Yeta that the woman was *agoraphobic*, a condition in which a person was afraid of open spaces. Still, *agoraphobia* didn't explain the unhealthy and psychotic storage of urine.

Strangely, they never bothered to claim their belongings. After a month, Pol told some workmen to put their things out for trash collection. Some needy neighbors helped themselves to whatever they could use. By the time the trash collectors came around, there was nothing to collect.

****

Apart from the few bad apples, 99% of their tenants were conscientious persons who paid their rents on time, kept their units clean and were friendly and neighborly to the other tenants.

One of their tenants in Cape Coral, Florida, has spent his own money to plant over 200 trees and bushes in a dramatic and spectacular design! He has stayed in the house for six years and has spent at least $20,000 to date in beautifying his residence. He maintains and nurtures his gardens as if he owns them. Peter Bailey is an unusual and a highly valued tenant!

Peter Bailey used different colors of mulches to delineate the pathways

Peter Bailey's landscaping

Peter Bailey in front of his rented house

Chapter Eleven.
Incredible Investment Returns

After a cosmetic renovation of each of their fifty apartments, the novice landlords raised the rents to their fair market value. Because the apartments were newly renovated, they were as good as new and could compete favorably with the other residential offerings in the city.

After all the fifty units had been rented out, then Yeta marveled at how much money was coming in! Every month, over $33,000 was coming in as income. The income was over $372,000 a year. She had never seen that kind of cash flow before in her life! Since the investments were heavily leveraged, virtually every dollar that came in was profit!

Their 1983 tax returns showed the income and expenses of each property:

Catherine St.

Income:	$41, 500

Expenses:

Taxes:	1919
Mortgage Interests	1717
Depreciation	1300
Other expenses	910

Total expenses	6,756
Net income	34,744

Ivy Hall:

Income:	99,200
Taxes:	1928
Mortgage Interest	1617
Depreciation	1800
Other expenses	2003

Total expenses	7,348
Net Income	91,852

Chester Ave, # 1

Income:	40,350
Expenses:	
Taxes	1512
Mortgage Interest	1680
Depreciation	1300
Other expenses	1178

Total expenses:	5670
Net income:	34,680

Chester Ave., # 2.

Income:	41,070
Expenses:	
Taxes	1733
Mortg Interest	1790
Depreciation	1500
Other expenses	2067

Total expenses:	7090
Net income:	33,980

325 11th St.
Income: 21,600

Expenses:

Taxes:	1895
Mortg. Interest	2614
Depreciation	1300
Other expenses	501

Total expenses:	6310
Net income:	15,290

10th St.
Income: 77,500

Expenses:

Taxes	1964
Mortg. Interest	2335
Depreciation	1800
Other expenses	1071

Total expenses:	7170
Net income:	70,330

Cedar Ave, # 1 & # 2

Income: 84,300

Expenses:

Taxes	2003
Mortg.Interest	2224
Depreciation	1750
Other expenses	788

Total expenses:	6765
Net income:	77,535

Based on the figures cited above, Yeta's and Pol's new venture netted them $358,411 for the first year. These were phenomenal returns! The returns would increase as they raised the rents every year by at least five percent. They took tremendous risks in originating short term loans that would balloon in four to seven years. They had no idea when the deep recession would end. They gambled heavily and won! It was just luck!

In January 1984, the loan of the apartment building where they lived became due. For the first time, they went to a commercial bank to refinance the loan. The clerk processing the application initially rejected the application on the grounds that they were not earning enough money to justify a $70,000 loan.

Pol gathered all their financial records and insisted on seeing and talking to the bank president. Pol patiently explained where the income was coming from. He showed the bank president their 1983 tax returns and the tax returns of the previous two years. The bank president even said, "As I see it, you're making too much money. I wish I have your cash flow."

The bank president advised the clerk to approve the new loan of $70,000 and to expedite the closing of the refinancing.

The refinancing of 325 11th St. was an important hurdle to clear successfully. It meant that they could refinance all the other properties when the loans became due. This was the first tangible proof that their investment scheme worked as they had planned it!

The unexpected bonanza in the investment returns tempted Pol to increase their inventory of buildings. He wanted to purchase much larger buildings. They started looking at a 65-unit building. Then, they even looked at a 100-unit property that simply overwhelmed Yeta! She didn't have the patience to inspect so many apartments in one day. She understood that it was necessary to see and analyze every single apartment so as to plan the renovations properly. Every apartment unit had its peculiarities and needs. Since the apartments were occupied, they had to plan carefully where the renovation would start and what the sequence of renovation would be. It would be financially responsible to limit the renovations to one or two floors at a time.

In spite of her mild protest, Pol made an offer on an 85-unit dilapidated building. The seller was a corporation in New York and was asking $1,800,000 in cash. Pol offered $1,300,000 as an initial offer, contingent on seller financing. He was prepared to go up to $1,500,000. The corporation turned down the offer and refused to finance the sale.

Pol suddenly realized that negotiating with an impersonal corporation was very difficult, if not impossible, to do. He was used to a face-to-face negotiation but the men he was talking to on the phone treated him as a nobody. He realized that he was out of his league! He needed to learn how to deal with corporations, especially with the big ones.

Meanwhile, Yeta was feeling anxious and afraid that owning large properties would overextend their resources! She was taking care of the book keeping and was already being overwhelmed by paper work! She knew that owning more properties would mean much more responsibilities. She was feeling burnt out and wanted out of the business! She wanted to retire somewhere where the weather was warm. She wanted to stop her husband from expanding the business!

This time, will Yeta leave Pol?

Chapter Twelve.
Early Retirement

Yeta suspected that Pol wanted to be rich and would try to persuade her to go along with his bigger vision of the business! She understood that an immigrant, like him, wanted to prove to the world that a foreign-born man can fulfill his dreams and be a successful investor! As a granddaughter of European Jewish immigrants, she had directly observed how some of her relatives became multi-millionaires.

She had an uncle, by the name of Leo, who made millions in manufacturing shopping carts. He started making a living by selling scraps of iron from a large bulky shopping cart. One day, he figured out that if he designed a smaller cart that shoppers could push around in a grocery store, their lives would be easier. And, of course, he would make millions of dollars in the process.

Leo had died a while ago but his heirs were still making millions from his simple invention. Yeta also had relatives in Toronto, Canada, who also became very rich.

Still, she didn't share her husband's ambitions! She didn't want to be rich; she just wanted to have enough money to pay her bills. The more she observed his inordinate drive, the more she distanced herself from him. She had suffered so much financial strain with her late husband, Sheldon, who juggled his cash flow to make partial payments to creditors. There were creditors who unexpectedly showed up at her door, demanding full payment. She felt embarrassed and ashamed for her incapacity to pay them.

She was very concerned that Pol might unduly stretch their financial resources to the point of owing many more creditors. She knew she was a conservative who wanted to limit her financial involvement to what was sure and safe. She felt that what they had achieved, thus far, was safe and manageable. She didn't want to change the status quo.

Moreover, she was getting fed up with some of her tenants. One tenant, Richard, habitually left one hour messages on her tape, griping and arguing about little things. With fifty units to keep tenanted, the pressure to keep all the tenants happy and contented was getting on her nerves!

Since she kept the books and the money, she knew there was more than enough money around to walk away from the business. They could ask a property management company to manage the business for them. If the management turned out to be inept, then they would put the properties for sale, two properties at a time.

****

In March 1985, Yeta received a real estate promotion from Lehigh Acres, a small community, southeast of Ft. Myers, in southwest Florida. The developer of the community sent two free plane tickets to Tampa, Florida. From Tampa, a private bus would take them down to Lehigh Acres, about eighty miles away. There were about sixty other potential buyers who came from different cities in the USA.

A salesman made about an hour and a half sales presentation just to two of them regarding home sites and time shares in their development. The longer the salesman talked, the less impressed they were about his skills as a salesman. They were not interested at all in the Lehigh properties.

They were not impressed by the community because it was not on water. They left to rent a car so they could see as much of the coastal region as they could see on their own. If they bought anything in southwest Florida, it had to be as close as possible to the Gulf of Mexico and preferably on water.

They drove to <u>Naples</u> and went to an open house in <u>Port Royal</u>, where <u>every house was on water</u>. Naples was nice and beautiful, but too expensive! A home site alone would already cost half a million dollars! Besides, they didn't want to live in a community where their neighbors might mistake them for a pool cleaner or a maid.

They drove up to Ft. Myers and drove along <u>McGregor Boulevard</u>, which was lined on both sides with Royal Palms. The Boulevard was beautiful and impressive. They passed by the house of the famous inventor, <u>Thomas Edison</u>. Hundreds of tourists were walking in line and listening to several tour guides.

The Riverfront was awesome, but again too expensive! They were sure they couldn't afford a Riverfront property. <u>Ft. Myers</u> is an old city on the bank of the Caloosahatchee River but most of the housing stock was old, plain and off-water.

They decided to check into a motel on the Tamiami Trail, south of Ft. Myers, and planned to return to Tampa the next morning.

In the evening, Pol went down to the ground floor of the motel to fetch some ice for his nightly alcoholic drink. In the room was a real estate brochure about <u>Cape Coral</u>, a city that was not in their road map. He leafed through the brochure and found some interesting displays of contemporary houses with affordable prices, like $60,000, $70,000 and 100,000!

There was an eye catching advertisement that said, "Four year old home on a wide canal, direct access to the Gulf of Mexico, boat davits, swimming pool with creepy crawly. Only $91,000."

Pol showed the advertisement to Yeta and said, "Why don't we take a quick look at this unknown community before returning to Tampa. All the houses being advertised are quite cheap. It must be a crime infested place."

"That's a good idea. Thus far, I feel like we have wasted our time coming down here. Thus far, we have not seen anything that looked good and was reasonably priced."

"I completely agree with you. Perhaps, looking for a good place to live takes a lot of time of studying, meeting real estate salesmen, understanding property values and a million other things."

"I think you're right. That is why we should go to Cape Coral and form our own opinions about a lot of things. Besides, we need to get more cash from American Express at around nine and then we can go to Cape Coral. Our plane for Philadelphia won't leave until two in the afternoon."

In the American Express office, Pol asked a female clerk for directions to the Cape. To their surprise, she responded defensively as if there was an implied insult in the request for direction.

She said, "You are now on College Parkway, which will take you directly to the Cape. Go westward until you reach a bridge. Cross the bridge and you're already in Cape Coral.

"By the way, when you asked me about Cape Coral, were you asking me about the restrictions? I live there and I like all the restrictions!"

She seemed belligerent and Pol didn't want to fuel her anger! Still, he was curious about the restrictions and proceeded to ask, "What are the restrictions?"

"The Cape is a highly restricted city. Residents are not allowed to keep trucks and boats on their driveways. They have to mow their lawns virtually every week during summer and they can't plant trees in the easement and so on."

"As you can see, we are a mixed couple; would we be allowed to live there if we decide to do so?"

"Of course, yes! The community is not racist."

"Yeta is Jewish. Will she be allowed to live there?"

"Yes, of course. I myself have many Jewish friends!"

"Why did you appear defensive when I asked you how to get to Cape Coral?"

"I'm sorry if I came across as defensive; I wasn't aware I was doing that. Perhaps, I have been defending the Cape from Ft. Myers residents who tend to criticize what they call, derisively as, 'The other side of the river, which meant that it was the bad side.' When they use that description, they use it as a put down! When I ask them if they had ever been to Cape Coral, they usually answer, 'No! And I have no intention of visiting it.' Then, I ask them, 'Why criticize a community you don't even know?' That is when they shut up!"

"Why do you think the Ft. Myers' residents bad mouth your city?"

"I think because they envy us! My city is new and very clean. There are no poor neighborhoods there. In contrast, Ft. Myers is an old and decaying city in many places. They have a bad neighborhood called, Dunbar. Hence, they are afraid the Cape will surpass their city. Frankly, the Cape had already surpassed Ft. Myers at least ten years ago!"

"Thank you for the information. From now on, I'll ignore any criticism from Ft. Myers residents."

"Please, do that!"

They crossed the Cape Coral Bridge and, quickly, they stopped at a traffic light on Del Prado. They could continue to go westward and stay on Cape Coral Parkway; or they could turn right and go north on Del Prado. For no reason at all, Pol decided to turn left and went south.

Del Prado gradually and gracefully turned to the right and it became Eldorado. The left turn proved to be interesting! Every home they saw was quite expensive and was well kept. The lawns were well manicured. Every house had about eighty feet of frontage and the houses were about thirty feet apart. Almost every house had a swimming pool. And there were boats on elevators or hanging from davits. Cape Coral was not what Pol had imagined; it was not a crime-ridden community at all. They felt perfectly safe driving around. The traffic on Eldorado was almost non-existent. Even on Del Prado, which was a main road, the traffic was very light.

The Cape Coral Bridge viewed from Cape Coral

There was a "for sale" sign on one of the <u>finger streets</u>. Indeed, the streets looked like long fingers because they were long and narrow. Next to the finger streets were <u>finger canals</u> that were navigable. As it actually turned out, the house that was for sale was on a wide lake called Bimini Lake. The Lake led to a wide canal that also led to the Gulf of Mexico.

The owner was also a real estate agent. She was asking $104,000 for a large three bedrooms, two baths, two car garage, a swimming pool and boat davits. There were two mature mango trees with large fruits in the back yard.

They found out from the seller that every house in the area was either on a wide navigable canal or on a lake.

Pol could see that Yeta was really interested in the house and with everything she was looking at. For her, the buying points for the house were the mango trees, the swimming pool, the Lake and the boat davits. She had owned a power boat in Barnegat Light, New Jersey, where she and her late husband had a second home. The home prices were obviously affordable! Coming from Philadelphia where a house on a big body of water could cost over a million, the $104,000 house on a big lake was undervalued!

However, they were not ready to make an offer. So, they resumed their tour of Eldorado but the road abruptly ended in a large canal. The street, on the other side of the canal, was still Eldorado, which meant that in the future, there would be a bridge connecting the streets.

They turned around and drove north on Interstate 75 to Tampa. In the afternoon, they boarded their plane for Philadelphia.

Both of them were highly impressed with whatever little they had seen of Cape Coral. The community was young and vibrant. From Pol's point of view, however, they were not ready to retire and relocate. They would, of course, consider the Cape when it was time to stop working.

The fishing pier at the Cape Coral Yacht Club

In retrospect, however, Yeta had already found her new community for retirement. She would find a way to buy a house there, retire and enjoy her new life of leisure!

From the real estate brochure Pol had given her, Yeta sent further inquiries from several brokers. She specified: waterfront, three bedrooms, two baths, two car garage, swimming pool and an excellent neighborhood. She did this without consulting with Pol. She had already made up her mind to hand over their real estate business to Ruth Miller, her long time friend.

In a couple of weeks, she received a reply from a broker named, Virgil Dwinenil. Virgil wrote, "This is a rare opportunity to own a home right on a mile-wide Caloosahatchee River. The large house has an oversized dock with an Indian chickee hut over the dock. The dock and chickee would extend your living area over the River, which is a unique way of living even in southwest Florida! This is a foreclosure situation. The asking price is only $139,500. Hurry and make an offer. This property will sell quickly!"

Yeta asked Pol to call Virgil and negotiate the purchase of the house. This request shocked him because he didn't know she was corresponding with brokers in Florida. And, buying a house that they hadn't even seen was not only risky but probably stupid! Nevertheless, he could tell that Yeta was in earnest! Her facial expression and the tone of her voice were saying, "Buy me this house or I'll kill you!"

He suspected that there was a very serious conflict brewing between them!

"Yeta, tell me the truth!" Pol said to her with trepidation! "What is happening here? Are you planning to leave me?"

"No, Pol! That would be inconceivable! I love you very much; I'll never leave you! You are the best thing in my life! I should have talked to you sooner. I've reached the point of being burnt out emotionally! I feel that if I don't leave Philadelphia, I'll either go crazy or become physically ill! I think we should hand over the properties to Ruth Miller for management and take an early retirement!"

The Cape Coral Regional Library

"I'm disturbed to hear you talk this way! I had no idea you're fed up with the business!

"On the other hand, if you feel we should retire early, we have built up enough equity on our properties and we can afford to retire. When we decide to sell them, we should be able to enjoy an early retirement!"

"I have been thinking this way for a while but, somehow, I have not mustered enough courage to bring it up with you until now!"

"This is a new idea and I have to get used to it! Come to think of it, I would love being retired especially to a warm climate like Florida. All right! I'll call Virgil right now."

"Pol, let us buy the property and if we don't like it or if we don't want to live in Florida, we can rent it out or sell it for a profit. But, it seems to me that this house is like a dream home! You told me that you grew up on the bank of a river. Well, if we buy this house, you'll be living on the bank of another river and you'll relive your childhood again!"

The Riverfront house viewed from the street

"That's true. All right! We're at a point in our lives when we have more options. What concerns me now is the proper management of our rental properties. I have read some *caviats* from some investment gurus that nobody can manage your properties for you."

"I believe that, too. Let us think ahead and figure out what we will do in case Ruth Miller's property managers mismanage our properties. What do you think we should do then?"

"That would be the time to sell them. But for tax purposes, we should sell no more than two buildings in one year."

"I agree; but what should we do with the proceeds?" Yeta asked with some concern!

"That is a good question but I have no answers. I think we should consider not only the best investment instruments but also the easiest. After all, we will be retired and we shouldn't be working too hard any more!"

"That is absolutely true. What keeps coming up in my mind is the stock market. I suggest that you do some studying about securities investments. If you know what you're doing, there is a lot of money to be made in the stock market."

View of the house from the river

"I think you have a good point there. But, both of us should be studying the same field."

"Not necessarily. I suggest that you invest in the stock market; I'll invest in mutual funds, which of course also deal with the stock market. I think mutual funds are less affected by market volatility."

"I honestly don't know, Yeta. But, I'll study everything there is to learn about the stock market. I'll have a more intelligent response in six months. Still, it's good that we are thinking along the same lines of thought. I agree with your proposal but contingent on what I'll learn during the next year or so. You concentrate on mutual funds and I'll concentrate on the stock market! Now, I'll call Virgil."

****

Pol called Virgil and asked him, "Virgil, how much was the last sale on the same block in Cape Coral?"

"Sal, give me a few minutes to look up the Multiple Listing Service. I'll call you right back."

After about fifteens, he called back. "Sal the last sale took place less than a month ago and it was for $150,000."

"Was the square footage of the house about the same as what you're selling to us?"

"No sir! The house had only 1700 square feet because it had only two bedrooms. Furthermore, it didn't have a pool. Whereas, the house I'm selling to you has 2350 square feet and it has a swimming pool and a large dock, which you can incorporate into your living area because it has a chickee hut on the dock. You can use the dock for fishing and crabbing. You can install a swing, a table and chairs under the chickee. You may even build a workshop under the chickee."

"That is a favorable comparison! Would you say that this house you're selling to us is under priced?"

"It appears that way, sir!"

"Virgil, will you send us some photos of the house and the surrounding areas, as soon as possible?"

"Of course, I will. You should get them in a couple of days."

View of the chickee hut, towards the left, and the mile wide river

"Thank you, Virgil. You have been very informative and helpful."

"Thank you also for responding to my letter. I think we can do business together and make a little money!"

****

The photos arrived early in the morning, two days after the call, as Virgil had promised. Pol received the package but gave it to Yeta. He went back to sleep!

Yeta spread the photographs on a large table and arranged them in a sequence. She looked for the photo of the house from the street. Then, she looked for the photo of the entrance of the house, followed by the vestibule, the living room, the kitchen, the great room, the master bedroom, master bathroom, the second bedroom, the laundry room, the third bedroom, then out to the swimming pool and down to the dock and under the chickee hut. She examined the photos of the River and the sailboats and the power boats navigating the channels close to the dock.

Yeta imagined herself walking through all the places shown in the photographs. She had already moved to Cape Coral, mentally! She became excited and couldn't wait to move to her new house on the River!

A volks wagon car/boat

As soon as Pol woke up, she asked him to start the negotiations immediately! So, Pol made his first offer of $120,000. He first called Virgil and made the offer verbally. Then, he followed the phone call with a telegram. The counter offer was a prompt repetition of the asking price of $139,500. The seller was clearly saying, "You should raise your offer and watch how I react!"

The next day, he sent another offer of $125,000 and received a prompt counter offer of $135,000. He could tell that the seller was motivated to sell and was willing to negotiate fairly. There was only $10,000 separating the seller from the buyer.

Three days later, Pol sent another offer of $127,000 and received a prompt counter offer of $132,000. By making a small increment of $2000, Pol was telling the seller that he wanted to buy the house for less than the asking price. Furthermore, the counter offer told him that the seller would settle for less money.

Pol purposely slowed down the negotiation to communicate the message that he wasn't an eager or desperate buyer!

His stalling tactics, however, infuriated Yeta who said to him, "I'll kill you if you lose this house for me!"

"I won't lose it, Yeta, because I know that the listing of the house was not published in the Multiple Listing service because Virgil told me so. I know that nobody else is making a negotiation with the selling broker. Virgil had told me that the listing broker, Ken Randall, wanted to buy the house for his own use. Hence, I know that I'm not competing with anybody else except with the broker who is short of cash. Randall was trying to sell some of his properties but nothing was moving for him."

"Are you telling me that Randall was keeping the listing unpublished for his own benefit?"

"It is illegal and unethical, but obviously, it is being done by Randall. If the state real estate commission should find out about it, he could be disciplined and even jailed for it. He is not being fair to the seller."

"Do you think Randall purposely listed the house under market value?"

"It appears that way. Virgil admitted it. As potential buyers, we're in the position to take advantage of Randall's folly."

"Pol, are you being fair to the seller?"

"Under the circumstances, I'm as fair as anyone can be. It is fair to take advantage of a situation created by somebody else. I didn't put the seller in a weak position. However, I see his weakness and I'll take advantage of it. This is exactly what it means to negotiate fairly. You use whatever you know that would improve your position."

After the seller had gone down to $132,000, Pol knew that he could close the negotiation by making a final offer of $129,500. He gave the seller two days to accept or reject it. His offer had the additional condition that the buyers had ten days to physically inspect the house.

The seller accepted the final offer within two hours. They immediately booked a plane flight to Ft. Myers, Florida, which was just across the River from Cape Coral. In five days, they were inspecting the gorgeous house on the bank of the Caloosahatchee River.

While inspecting the house, two buyers, with full price offers, showed up and asked them what they had decided. By that time the buyers arrived in Cape Coral, the property had been finally listed in the Multiple Listing Service. Pol told them that they were definitely buying the house. The potential buyers looked very disappointed! They knew they had lost what could have been a rare "steal!"

Pol was happy with what he saw and was determined to go ahead with the purchase. He had already decided to buy a Saroca sailboat and would install boat davits for it. He was also considering the installation of a powerboat elevator.

Yeta, however, had some misgivings. The house was not exactly as she had imagined it! The water in the pool was less than a foot deep and was full of algae. It looked disgusting! The grounds were full of weeds. And, she didn't like the green color of the house. The previous owners were Irish-Americans and emerald was everywhere!

She felt better when Pol said to her, "Look, sweetheart, whatever you don't like, we'll change and improve. We'll hire a pool man to take care of the dirty pool. And, we'll hire a landscaper to take care of the grounds. I think this house is a gem in the rough! Its sterling qualities will show off after we redo the flooring and redo the covering around the pool area. Indoor/outdoor green carpeting doesn't enhance the pool at all. "

The Indian Chickee hut on the oversize dock

"What do you think we should use as flooring?"

"Yeta, that is really your area of expertise. As usual, I give you the liberty to choose the materials and colors that would enhance the property. Let me just share some of my thoughts on the matter. How about using tiles for the living room, kitchen, dining room and the great room?"

"I like that idea. How about the bedrooms? Should we also use tiles?"

"Don't you think that they would be warmer if carpeted?"

"I'll think about it. This afternoon, let us visit a tile store. I'm crazy about Mexican tiles."

"That is fine with me. I'm just concerned that Mexican tiles might be too expensive."

****

They thought that the closing of the sale would take about three months since it took that long in Philadelphia. The processing of a mortgage was what took a long time. They could return to Philadelphia and close the sale by mail.

In fact, the closing of the sale was much faster than they had expected! The actual seller turned out to be a lending company, which was a subsidiary of General Electric, a multi-national conglomerate. Pol had been intimidated by an impersonal corporation in Philadelphia. Little did he suspect that he had been negotiating the purchase of their house with a multi-national corporation, General Electric, no less!

The versatile Saroca sailboat. It had a mainsail and a jib, paddles, oars and a small 3 horsepower engine

The company had already checked out their credentials and their credit ratings. The lending company, which had foreclosed on the previous owner, was prepared to lend them a mortgage <u>loan of $103,600</u>, which was 80% of the cost of the house, amortized for 30 years at 8%.

The lender would also <u>wave the closing costs</u> if they signed the papers in three days.

They signed the closing papers and also signed five more contracts with the different contractors: a painter, a pool man, a floor tiler, a roofer and a landscaper. They signed several blank checks and left them with Virgil so he could pay the workmen every Friday.

They left for Philadelphia on June 15, 1985 to pack their belongings and prepared to relocate to Cape Coral, Florida.

They made an arrangements with Ruth Miller, Yeta's old friend, to take over the management of their rental properties. Ms Miller opened a property management division to her real estate sales business precisely to accommodate Yeta and Pol.

Yeta and Pol had some misgivings about the lack of experience of the management division. Only the future would tell if their management personnel were competent or not.

View of the dock, chickee hut, boat channels, boat elevator
and a new boat

By July 25, 1985, they were basking in the Florida sun and enjoying their life of leisure in a Riverfront house. Even though Pol was initially against early retirement, he completely changed his mind as soon as he saw the house on a mile-wide Caloosahatchee River. As he watched the sailboat regatta on the River and the thousands of powerboats navigating the channels just five feet away from his dock, he fell in love with Riverfront living. A little more than a month earlier, he was sure they couldn't afford to buy a house on the River. What they didn't think was possible became a reality!

To make sure that they could afford their early retirement, he quickly computed their net worth. It was approximately a million and a half dollars! That was enough money to support their retirement, however long they lived. He said to himself, "I'm only 54 years-old but I no longer have to work for a living because we have accumulated enough wealth to support our retirement!"

For the first time in his life, he felt truly free and happy!

Before he could play and explore the waterways of southwest Florida, Pol had to do a lot of work with the landscaping of the grounds. The previous owner, James Walsh, was a builder but had become financially bankrupt. Angry with his financial failure, he wasn't motivated to maintain the grounds and the landscaping. He also neglected the swimming pool. The lawn had been sodded with bahia grass but the grass had died and the area was covered with tall weeds!

Their 24 foot powerboat, a Cabin Cruiser

Pol didn't want to re-sod the lawn. In the Philippines, most residents didn't keep lawns. Either they planted vegetable gardens and fruit trees or they made rock gardens. He preferred to make rock gardens. He also wanted to make meandering pathways around the house.

He figured out that if he made meandering pathways, the footpaths would naturally create "islands", which he could turn into plant beds. If he then brought in some rocks and arranged them artistically, he had his rock gardens all done!

It so happened that rocks were all over the whole city of Cape Coral. Before the city was developed, the elevation of the land ranged from swamps, which could be six feet below sea level, to about four feet of dry land. The developers of the city wanted to raise the elevation of the land to at least seven feet above sea level to make the home sites more suitable for development. The developers figured out that if they dug deep and wide canals and lakes and dredged the Caloosahatchee River, they had enough soil and rocks to raise the elevation by three to five feet.

First, dredging the River, along the banks, immediately created deep navigable channels for large yachts to sail to the Gulf of Mexico and around the world. The dredging process uncovered <u>fossilized coral rocks</u> and <u>boulders</u>. The ancient fossils were readily visible to the naked eye. Pol used dollies, wheel barrows and hoists to bring the rocks and smaller boulders to his rock gardens. He piled the rocks in different patterns. He also carved faces on some larger rocks.

The new rock gardens

Yeta stands on the bridge. Notice the water under the bridge

One day, there was a small "no name storm" that uprooted some pilings on the River. One of the floating pilings became lodged against the pilings of Pol's dock. Using ropes and a hoist, he pulled the piling to the dock. He cut the 20-foot piling into two sections and carved two totem poles.

He used an electric chain saw to carve out the basic features. He had never used a chain saw before and it scared him so!

On the first piling, he carved an alligator, an owl and an eagle holding a tarpon fish. These animals represented the wild life in the region. On the second piling, he carved four faces representing the four races: black, white, brown and yellow.

He installed the totem poles near the steps, at the back of the house, leading to the dock and the chickee hut.

Some friends and neighbors immediately labeled Pol an artist, which he simply rejected! In his mind, he was just playing and making frivolous things. To him, an artist was one who had trained in art academies.

Then, he dug a meandering shallow ditch in front of the house, which simulated the Caloosahatchee River. He built a small bridge across his "River," which he called the Edison Bridge. At the end of his River, he dug a pond, which was his idea of Lake Okeechobee, the twenty-five mile long by forty mile wide Lake in central Florida. Around their mail box, he piled a high mound of rocks, which he called the "Rocky Mountain!"

This pathway is located in the back, between the swimming pool and the dock

Pol was having a ball making fanciful assemblages out of found objects. He assembled found things on every rock garden and thought they were funny! Passersby and some neighbors thought they were artistic. So, they called him an artist. Again, he rejected the designation because his second grade teacher in the Philippines had told him he would never be an artist because his hand writing was crude and scratchy.

In 1998, Dr. Charles Watkins, the director of the Appalachian Cultural Museum of the Appalachian State University in Boone, North Carolina and Dr. Rao Aluri, the publisher of Parkway Publishers, commissioned Pol to write a book about his artwork. These two men had become acquainted with Pol's art because he had created several pieces around his house in Boone, North Carolina. Starting in 1991, when they built their mountain house, Pol had made several outdoor sculptures of different sizes around their house.

However, his primary symbolic artworks were the pathways because he considered himself, first and foremost, as a gardener.

In April 1999, "My Taoist Vision of Art" came off the press.

Expecting some local publicity in Florida for his new book, Pol decided to do a large mosaic wall on the retaining wall on the back of their property. The wall was 5 feet by 80 feet. The primary theme was the meandering Caloosahatchee River that ran through his backyard. The other minor themes were the Taoist Yin-Yang symbols, a tarpon fish biting its tail, large spiral movements that represented waves and spontaneous designs suggested by natural forces such as storms and hurricanes!

The mosaics became popular to the boaters; it was something to look at and figure out. It became a boating destination for some boaters.

Chief Calusa, made out of PVC and concrete

****

After he finished the landscaping, he started playing with his "Saroca," the most versatile sailboat ever designed in Scandinavia. It was imported from Sweden. It was primarily a sailboat but it had an auxiliary engine with three horse power. They paddled the boat for exercise. They also rowed it for heavier exercise and faster speed. They used it to chug around and looked at the canal-front and river-front houses.

One day, they decided to visit the Yacht Club of Cape Coral by operating the auxiliary engine. What they thought was a twenty minute trip, turned out to be an hour and twenty minute ordeal as they navigated against a strong Gulf wind. That belabored trip convinced them to buy a twenty-four foot powerboat. Pol had already foreseen that they might have to buy a powerboat because of the vast expanse of the River and the Gulf of Mexico.

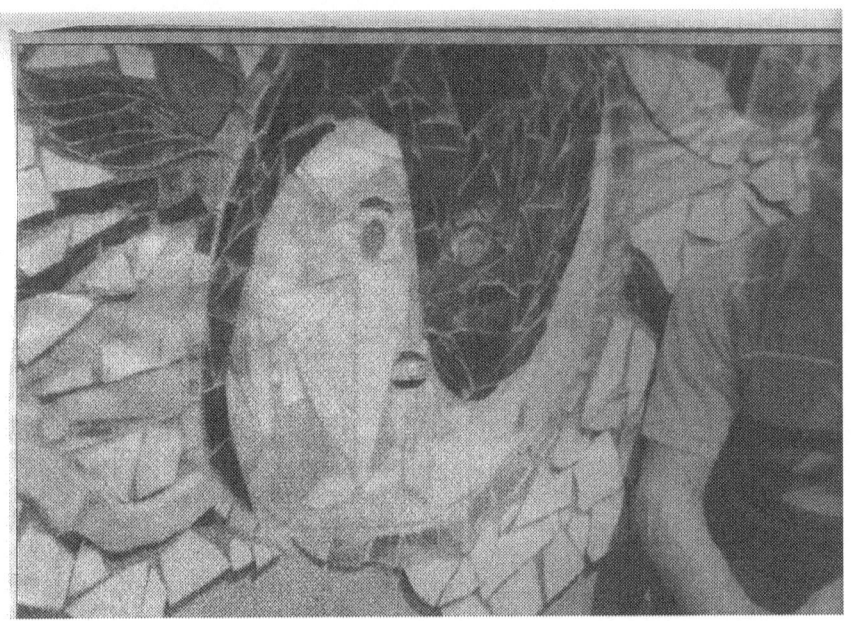

A small portion of the 80 foot long mosaic on the retaining wall

The powerboat allowed them to explore the many barrier islands along the coastline of the Gulf of Mexico. They were able to visit Cabbage Key and its funky restaurant, which the famous mystery writer, Mary Roberts Rhinehart, used to visit. They were also able to visit Cayo Costa and many other barrier islands.

The boat also allowed them to make a long trip to Palm Beach by navigating the whole length of the Caloosahatchee River, through Lake Okeechobee, to Palm Beach and West Palm Beach.

Life was becoming an endless adventure and Pol was enjoying every minute of it!

Chapter Thirteen.
Time Shares

After officially declaring their Florida residency, Yeta and Pol applied for a Florida driver's license and also obtained a Florida car registration. Within a month, they started receiving solicitations to time shares presentation. For a free dinner, a free television set or a free set of matching suit cases, the potential time share buyers listened to a 90-minute sales presentation.

TS in Sanibel Island, Florida

For those not cognizant of "Time Shares," (henceforth, TS), they are a fraction of equity ownership to lavish vacation resorts. In the beginning, TS were only "right to use," as opposed to "right to own" types of public offerings. The right to use, as the expression implies, is not a property ownership. It was like checking into a hotel for the night and paying $60 for the right to use the room. The "user" paid for the use of the facilities, for the duration of time.

In contrast, equity ownership bestows a deed for a fraction of the real estate value of the property. The TS owner may sell it for a certain amount, if he chooses to do so. When the owner dies, the TS unit goes to his heirs, as instructed by his will and testament.

For a long time, TS ownership was parceled out into a unit of time, which was <u>one week</u>. The assumption was that the vacationers preferred a whole week of relaxation and enjoyment, instead of just a day or two. There was another assumption that the likely buyers were families and a family vacation needed at least a week of R&R.

Likewise, in the beginning, the time frame for using a TS was for a <u>fixed time</u>. Hence, if you bought a week at the beginning of December, the owners must use the facilities on the same date every year. If the owners failed to use their unit, for whatever reason, they forfeited their privilege to use it for that year. Fix time was too rigid and it needed to evolve into something more "user friendly."

TS in California

Then, the TS management changed the fixed time to <u>flexible time</u>, which allowed the <u>exchanges</u> of TS. Consequently, if you owned a week in December, you may exchange that week with someone's week in July or any other month.

To facilitate exchanges, there were <u>two exchange</u> agencies: RCI and Interval International (II). For a small fee, the owner registered his TS with an agency and exchanged it anywhere in the world, at any time he chooses.

To make the exchanges <u>fairer,</u> the resorts and the seasons of the year were assigned a specific color. **Red** was for the most desirable times such as Christmas and holidays; **white** was for less desirable times and places; and **blue** for the least desirable.

There were also <u>different sizes of facilities</u>. TS units may be <u>efficiencies</u> with a sofas bed and one bathroom; <u>one bedroom</u> with sofa bed and one bath; <u>two bedrooms</u> with sofa bed and <u>two bathroom</u> or even <u>three bedrooms</u> a sofa bed and <u>three bathrooms,</u> etc. Based on their own experience with exchanges, the most popular units are two bedrooms, a sleep sofa and two bathrooms. The most active TS users are retirees who prefer to sleep in a separate bed because of someone snoring, sleep walking, talking in their sleep and so on.

If your TS is red and you have two bedrooms and two baths, you should be able to exchange easily with similar TS. If you have blue and you want to exchange with red, your chances of successful exchanges are either nil or very poor. This is called "trading up."

However, if you are pressed for time and other constraints, you might not mind to exchange your red for a blue or a white. That is feasible. You might also exchange your two bedrooms for a one-bedroom or even an efficiency unit. It's your choice. This is called "trading down." The fastest way to secure an exchange is to trade down!

Resorts in certain states, like Florida and Hawaii, and cities like Las Vegas or Reno, Nevada, are all red. Hence, if you own a TS in these states or cities, you shouldn't have any trouble making fair and innovative exchanges.

Today, the new trend is to split the week into days. The TS industry has made exchanging easier by converting ownership into <u>points</u>. For example, a week's ownership in some Florida resorts may be converted to 46,000 points. Certain resorts in Florida may have 50,000 or more point conversion.

This point conversion was due to the new realization that many vacationers don't really want to stay in one place for a whole week. The point system allows the vacationer to stay in a resort for one day, which would cost him or her 6,572 points. If the vacationer wants to go to another facility in another state at another time, he or she can do so and stay just two or three days. This point system caters to frequent vacationers and travelers!

TS in the tropics

To make traveling easier and more convenient, the RCI TS agency has bought several hotels and motels in cities that accept points. For example, Days Inn and Ramada Inn now accept points as payment. Since points have cash value, more hotels will also accept points as payment. Of course, they also accept cash and credit cards. Hence, the point system has made TS as part of the daily currency. It has become as useful as cash or credit cards.

Recently, the author has learned that points could be used to rent cars and for taking cruises. It makes sense since points have dollar value.

Using TS for vacation is very luxurious but affordable. After buying a week or 50,000 points, you own the TS for life or in perpetuity. You can bequeath it to your heirs and it may stay in the family for generations.

While the cost of staying in hotels and motels keep rising, the cost of your TS is frozen at the purchase cost. TS is one way of motivating you to take a vacation every year in glamorous places that you can afford. Studies have shown that people who take vacations maintain their health better than those who do not take a break.

TS resorts are equivalent to four or five star hotels. They have all the amenities that you can imagine and they are located in places that are close to big bodies of water and close to various "theme parks."

****

The first time Yeta and Pol were exposed to TS was in Cancun, Mexico, in January 1979, while on their honeymoon. They were sunning on a beach when a sales man invited them to "An all you can drink tequila party." They didn't know that the free tequila was based on the assumption that they had to listen to a 90-minute sales presentation. Everything Pol had heard sounded good; even though he could barely remember signing the papers. The salesman made sure his tequila glass was always full. Getting the customer drunk was a calculated strategy!

TS in big cities like New York City

The TS contract gave them two weeks to rescind it if they changed their minds. Pol had some questions about owning properties in Mexico. He called the salesman, who was never available. He left several messages that were not returned. As a result, they voided their contract.

In November 1985, however, they were ready to buy a TS in Naples, Florida, thirty-five miles from their home in Cape Coral. Their primary reasons were (1) to own a TS that they could exchange with other owners anywhere in the world; (2) because the sale included a "charter membership," which included the use of all the facilities in the resort, including the use of sailboats and powerboats; and (3) because the TS was a closeout and was discounted by $5000.

The charter membership included weekly picnic on the Vanderbilt Beach, which served hamburgers, hot dogs and drinks. Charter membership gave them a chance to meet new friends. The one week TS cost them only $7,000. The original cost of the red TS week was $12,000.

Their first exchange was in Edisto Island in Georgia, just east of Savanna. They were interrupting their travel from Boone, North Carolina to Cape Coral, Florida. Their stop over in Edisto Island was to acclimatize their bodies to a warmer climate. When they left Boone in late October, the temperature was already freezing. In contrast, when they returned to Florida, the temperature would still be in the high 80 degrees. They hoped that a seven day exposure to the coastal heat would prepare their bodies to subtropical weather. The one week stop at the island seemed to have acclimatized their bodies to the warmer weather. Since the sojourn in Ediso Island worked perfectly for them and since there are several barrier islands off the coastlines of South Carolina and Georgia, they decided to make the stopover as an annual routine.

The following year, they exchanged with a Hilton Head Plantation resort, in South Carolina. The whole island had been divided into self-contained corporate developments, which they called Plantations. What they developed were not plants or crops but buildings. They had single family residences, multi-unit condominiums, times shares, banks, restaurants, golf courses, tennis courts and so on.

Still, the plantation metaphor alludes to the "ante bellum prosperity" that plantation owners in the south enjoyed. The whole Hilton Head Island looked lush, prosperous and exclusive!

TS promotions were all over the island. The promotions gave each customer a $50 certificate to an upscale restaurant to listen to their TS presentations. Since Yeta and Pol were still learning about TS, they attended about three more presentations but didn't buy anything.

The presentation at Marriot Hotel was the first time they heard about the point system, explained earlier. The Marriot Hotels created their own point system, with a complicated bonus incentives intended to entice the members to travel all year round. For example, if a member used 50,000 points, he automatically gets a bonus of 10,000 points. Every time he used 10,000 points, he received 1,000 more points.

In subsequent years, they exchanged with a resort in San Miguel Allende, in Mexico; with New Orleans, Louisiana; Las Vegas, Nevada and other interesting places.

In 1988, Avatar Properties, the biggest developer in the Cape Coral, proposed to exchange a TS week in Royal Poinciana, near Orlando, Florida, for their undeveloped home site in Cape Coral. They jumped at the opportunity to own another TS week in Orlando, near Disney World. It was a favorable exchange for them because their home site only cost them $4,000. To them, the Orlando TS was worth at least $20,000.

In January 2005, they used their Royal Poinciana TS. That was the time when a resort personnel informed them that they could convert their TS into a point system. Since Pol was already familiar with the system and believed that it was a better offering than the existing "weekly system," he agreed to the deal. Yeta, however, was not convinced especially since it would cost them $2,000 to convert. Eventually, she agreed to the deal but she still has her reservations.

Meanwhile, RCI agency has informed them that the conversion value of Royal Poinciana TS was 46,000 points; and, the Naples TS was also 46,000 points. The 92,000 points should be enough for a two-week Alaskan Cruise in 2006.

The point system has made TS more user-friendly and the author predicts that TS will become even more popular in the future!

Chapter Fourteen.
Stock Market Crash

Their initial misgivings with the Miller Management Company were quickly coming true! Every month, the amount of money the company was sending to Cape Coral was becoming less and less. By January 1986, the business was losing serious cash flow! The Miller "mis-management office" had a 42% vacancy rate! When they handed over the properties to Ruth Miller, there was zero vacancy.

They made an emergency trip in January to Philadelphia to find out what was causing the high vacancy. When they looked at the first vacant apartment at Chester Ave., they immediately understood why the vacant apartments couldn't be rented out. There were two broken windows in the loft apartment. The carpeting had burnt areas and was very dirty. The stove had not been cleaned and two burners were not working and the refrigerator was not operational.

As the saying goes, "No one can manage your properties for you. That may be true but the fact was that the management was simply ignorant and negligent! The people in charge had no idea what it meant to rent apartments. The actual vacancy during the last four month was 44 percent.

They strongly suspected that the negligence was intentional to force them to put the properties on the market for sale. There was more money on sales commissions than on rental commissions. They realized that, given the situation, they had to sell at least two of the properties.

Yeta had a private conference with Ruth Miller. She instructed her to list two properties in the University City for sale. Two weeks later, investors bought the two properties listed. Pol immediately bought blue chip stocks. And Yeta bought five mutual funds. Fortunately, they were riding a bull market and they felt like geniuses because their choices were appreciating in value every day. They felt economically secure because their investments were performing fantastically well!

Meanwhile, Yeta instructed Ms Miller to list two more buildings in the University City for sale. As soon as they received the money, Pol put money in <u>blue chips stocks</u>.

Then, suddenly in October 1987, the <u>market crashed to the ground for no valid reason</u>! They lost confidence in the advisory letters and also lost confidence in the integrity of the securities market. They liquidated all their portfolios. By the time they had sold all their holdings, they had lost over $500,000. Still, they felt liberated!

They decided to put what was left of their assets in an instrument they knew and trusted<u>: leveraged real estate</u>. They hired two builders to build rental houses from the ground up on home sites they had selected and purchased. They had chosen four different facades. Each house had three bedrooms, two baths, two car garages and measured 1350 square feet in air conditioned areas. The houses would be built in upscale areas and no more than two blocks away from water.

Their intended renters were young professional families with good jobs and older working couples who couldn't afford to buy their own homes. In three years, they had <u>built eighteen homes</u>. Each house had a $40,000 mortgage, amortized over 30 years.

They felt better about their new investments because they had the control of their portfolio and their money. They were convinced that, in time, they would recoup everything that they had lost in the stock market.

Two types of facades

Every house was absolutely new; and the houses were well tailored for the intended clientele. Since construction money was easy to borrow in 1987, they intended to put two houses on a <u>lease/purchase</u> <u>agreement.</u> Tenants who intended to own their homes, in the near future, could offer an <u>option money</u> of $5,000, which would be credited towards the sale when the tenants exercised their option to buy. This instrument was good for young couples who were saving money for a down payment. When they had saved enough money, then they could exercise their option.

Lease with option to buy was also good for the owners because it gave them the option money, which they could use for more investments. This investment instrument was flexible because there were other features, which could be included in the agreement. For example, to "sweeten" the agreement, the landlords may credit $50 or $100 of the monthly rent towards the purchase of the house in two or three years.

If the tenants failed to exercise the option within the agreed time, they forfeited the option money. The landlords may then offer the same house for another lease/purchase agreement. This was one way of making extra money on the same financial assets.

Another facade

The investors continued to offer lease/purchase agreements to their tenants but discontinued it after ten years. There was only a little profit in the whole scheme.

Chapter Fifteen.
The New Real Estate Schemes

Their experience in rental properties in Philadelphia taught them that managing multi-unit buildings was labor intensive and pressure laden! The repairs and maintenance of every unit was the responsibility of the owners. Pol learned quickly that if any job was small, tradesmen wouldn't work for him. He ended up doing his own repairs and maintenance. In the process, he learned at least twenty different handicrafts. He did carpentry, plumbing, electricity, painting, masonry, tiling, pressure cleaning, brick-laying, concrete work, glass repairs, air conditioning, roofing and so on!

They thought they had already retired in July 1985. Because they lost so much money in October 1987 market crash, they had to go back to work and recoup some of the losses. However, they didn't want to go back to do physical work. Psychologically, they no longer had the energy or the drive to do physical work. They would, of course, manage the properties but with the least effort and responsibilities.

For this reason, they decided to manage only single family houses, instead of apartment buildings. By owning only single family houses, they could pass on most of the minor repairs and maintenance to the tenants. What Pol had done was to <u>open accounts with several service companies</u> (plumbing, electricity, air conditioning, roofing and so on). He <u>authorized every tenant to call the companies for service</u> and to mention who their landlord was. This way, the services could be charged to the landlord.

Pol and Yeta have also employed a <u>super handy man, Randy Eckert</u>, who could do virtually anything and everything. Randy had been a builder in New Jersey and could do anything efficiently and quickly. He had done several jobs in their own home in Cape Coral and had prepared several rental houses for rent. He has been working for them for at least fifteen years and they trust him as an honest, reliable and reasonably affordable workman.

Some of their male tenants, like Ed Ewing, Ed Fereira, Bob Matucek and Mike Redden were also handy. They replaced parts of appliances, sent the receipts to Yeta and deducted the cost from their rent. This arrangement has worked remarkably.

The tenants might not realize it, but they are the ones who are paying the mortgages of the houses they live in. Every month, the mortgage debt of each house goes down and the equity of each property keeps going up. This is definitely a good and easy way to make a living. On the one hand, they are providing an important service to their tenants by providing them housing. At the same time, they are also feathering their own nest.

Meanwhile, they have diversified their assets. They have put some of their savings in a trust fund; they have opened four construction loans that pay as high as twelve percent; they bought several Certificates of Deposit; they also opened money market funds and an interest bearing checking account.

It took Yeta and Pol <u>over ten years to recoup their losses</u> in the stock market. They kept applying the same investment principles because they were sure they were essentially sound. Finally, <u>their net worth has been rising</u> handsomely!

Their new scheme was not as highly leveraged as their investments in Philadelphia but their debts were not as high. Moreover, they didn't have to insure the second mortgage. They decided not to bother with second mortgages. With much less debt, the cash flow of each house was more consistent. For this reason, each house was steadily appreciating in market value!

****

After the crash of the stock market in 1987, some out-of-state banks came to Cape Coral and were aggressively soliciting good clients. Plymouth Five Cents, from Boston, Ma, approved a <u>master plan</u> of lending money to them for whatever reason. Yeta and Pol were <u>pre-approved for loans,</u> as many as they wanted. If they decided to build a house, they simply called Vicky, the bank representative in Cape Coral and told her that they needed a construction loan for a house in Cape Coral. In one day, Vicky brought the paper work for the loan. All they had to do was sign the documents. The bank was so generous!

A speculation home

In January 1988, they entered into a partnership with a builder, Frank Nicotera and his marketing company, Key Design. Nicotera would build four speculative homes (spec-homes). Yeta and Pol would service the four construction loans and Key Design would market the houses. After each house had been sold, the proceeds would be divided three ways: one-third would go to the builder, one-third to Key Design and one-third to the investors.

By June 1988, the first house was finished and sold. They received $5000 as their portion of the profits. Their expenses were about $2000 and they made a small profit of $3000. It was a small amount of money but there was hardly any work involved. Their good credit history was making for them a small profit. They could earn an extra $12,000 to $15,000 every year with very little effort.

A spec home

By February 1989, the second and third houses were finished and sold. However, Nicotera didn't disburse their share of the profits because he suddenly went bankrupt! The fourth house was also finished but couldn't be sold because the banks had frozen all the Key Design's and Nicotera's assets.

Yeta and Pol had to decide how to deal with the construction loan of the fourth house. Strictly speaking, they should service the loan every month. Since the house was tied up in bankruptcy, servicing the loan would be tantamount to "casting pearls to swine." They decided not to service the loan and left the decision to the bank. By not servicing the loan, they were forcing the bank to foreclose on the property.

For six months, Yeta and Pol heard nothing from the bank. On the seventh month, the bank offered them a 40,000 mortgage, amortized over 30 years. The $40,000 mortgage was the amount of the construction loan. They accepted the offer because it meant that they were buying a $60,000 house for only $40,000. The $20,000 difference was their profit from the defunct partnership.

In spite of Nicotera's and Key Design's bankruptcy, Yeta and Pol still made some money. In December 2004, they sold the $40,000 house for $139,000. They made almost $100,000 just on one house! Now, that was a better profit!

The only adverse effects that the bankruptcy brought them were several <u>mechanics liens</u> that workers and suppliers filed on the fourth house in their futile attempt to recoup their own losses. There were ten liens that were later on withdrawn.

Assuming fraud on the part of Mr. Nicotera, the Mabulbuls sued Key Design and Nicotera. They paid Attorney Gail McDonald $5,000 as a retainer fee to file a legal suit and other legal formalities. Miss McDonald was certain the money in the account would cover the whole case.

After two weeks, however, McDonald billed Yeta and Pol for another $5,000 because the first retainer account had already been used up by lengthy phone calls from the other investors of Key Design. Since the callers were not her clients, she couldn't bill them for her time. She had to bill the Mabulbuls because they were her clients of record. In effect, she piggy-backed the callers costs on her clients' case.

Pol immediately fired McDonald as their lawyer and threatened to sue her for malpractice for unfairly charging them for services rendered to other clients who were not connected to them. They didn't expect to receive any refund but the move stopped any further billings.

In retrospect, when she found out that there were many more potential clients, she took the opportunity to file a class action suit against Key Design and Nicotera. The Mabulbuls didn't want to be part of an amorphous group. Moreover, by that time, they were no longer convinced that fraud was involved!

They found out that Nicotera and Key Design had built a good reputation of providing a legitimate investment outlet especially for senior citizens who had some money to invest. Frank Nicotera had been building "spec-homes" for five years. He entered into partnerships with investors, who provided construction funds. Nicotera built the houses and Key Design marketed the properties. The marketing department was headed by John Riflemacher and his wife, Doris, served as the secretary/treasurer. There were at least thirty investors and Nicotera was building at least 100 homes a year.

The Key Design partnerships were working smoothly until February 15, 1988. That week, Nicotera failed to pay his workers and failed to pay his suppliers. The whole machinery just ground to a halt! Without the weekly payment, the workers refused to work and the suppliers refused to deliver the supplies. Nicotera was forced to declare bankruptcy to protect himself from his creditors.

In retrospect, Nicotera and Key Design became bankrupt because the business operation was <u>under capitalized</u>. Nicotera was operating a business that had <u>only one week amount of</u> <u>disposable cash</u>. He was juggling cash from week to week. The operation worked until one day he was short of cash.

One investor was caught with fifteen unfinished homes that couldn't be sold. He also declared bankruptcy three months later. Yeta and Pol were caught with one finished house, which turned into a small bonanza for them. They were the only ones who didn't lose any money from the Nicotera/Key Design bankruptcy.

They had a chance to invest in "spec homes" with another builder, Paul Hubbard. Hubbard was from England, who called his company Trichon Builders. He built most of Yeta's and Pol's rental homes. A couple of times, they asked Paul to build for them "spec homes" that they could market themselves. It was an experimental venture to find out if they could generate extra income by speculation. Paul built about 65 homes a year and 90% of his construction was on speculation.

They paid their own advertisement and sent the customers to Paul's "spec homes." In effect, they were competing with their builder, which was not a healthy situation. After selling a couple of such "spec homes," they realized that there was little money to be made. The two "spec homes" only netted them about $8,000. It was too small a profit to justify the risks they were taking. The risk was in not selling the houses soon enough. Servicing the construction loans could eat up most of the profits.

Nevertheless, working with builders opened up another avenue of investment---<u>lending construction loans to builders</u>. Pol had learned from his tennis partner that McGregor Homes was soliciting some investors for construction loans at 12%. The builder, Bob Kroppa, used the home site and the house being built as the collateral for the loan. Pol's friend and tennis partner, John Hustle, had been lending Bob Kroupa several construction loans for the past ten years. John trusted him with over a million of his money.

They would later on lend more money to the same builder. They found out that this method of lending money was both safe and lucrative!

Chapter Sixteen.
Building a Summer Home

In spite of the heavy losses in the stock market, their credit rating was sufficiently sound to borrow $80,000 as construction loan to build a summer home in the Appalachian Mountains of North Carolina. Five years earlier, they had bought a condominium on King St., in Boone, North Carolina, for their own use in summer. They rented out the two-bedroom condo to students for nine months. They used it for three months during summer.

The 3 buildings that constituted the Daniel Boone Condo

They had chosen Boone, over many other towns and cities, because it was a "university town." They knew that a big university would raise the intellectual and cultural levels of the community as well as their own.

Appalachian State University (ASU) is so unique because of the long geographical isolation of the institution. When the university needed to provide housing to visiting dignitaries, speakers and lecturers, ASU constructed the Broyhill Inn primarily to provide lodging for the visitors. When the city needed electricity for the city residents and the students, ASU founded the New River Power and Light. The university provided exercise facilities not just for the students but for the public. The students needed a public transportation to go to their classes, so ASU bought a fleet of buses, which are called Appalcarts. The buses are free to both students and the public.

Recently, a private enterprise that provided exercise facilities to the public sued ASU for unfair competition. But, ASU was not at fault. It had been providing such services for over 100 years. One service that was recently terminated by ASU was laundry because of lawsuits from private businesses.

Even today, the university shows excellent movies at the Green Briar Theater for free. The Green Briar Theater is state-of-the-art facility with very comfortable leather seats and excellent sound and screen projection. These free offerings are open to the public. The ASU students have their own bowling lanes and billiard tables. The amenities provided by the university are unheard of even in the Ivy League Schools!

Yeta and Pol bought their condo at the Daniel Boone Condominium in 1986.

The condo was a large two bedrooms and two baths with balconies both in front and the back. It served their purposes until the middle of August 1990, when they decided to stay longer in Boone.

Fifty percent of the residents of the three buildings, that <u>comprised</u> the Daniel Boone Condo, were students. Most of the students went home for summer but they returned in October. Every night, there were loud parties in every building. Yeta couldn't sleep because of the party noise! She called the police to keep the kids better behaved. They kept their voices down only while the police was present. As soon as he left, they resumed their raucous behavior!

Yeta decided that the solution to her problem was to build a house away from the students. So, they started looking for a home site to build their new summer home. Fortunately, there was a home site available just half a block away. The land had been part of the Victorian Daniel Boone Hotel that had been demolished by the developers of the Daniel Boone Condominium. The large home site had been rezoned to eight lots. This meant that eight houses or a large building with eight apartments could be built on the same land.

Developers had made offers to buy the land for $50,000, subject to commercial rezoning. However, every time there was a hearing in the City Hall to rezone the home sites, hundreds of city residents showed up to protest the rezoning. The Boone residents wanted to stop commercial development in residential areas. Hence, the zoning board was forced to reject the change of zoning after every hearing.

Due to the public opposition, Jerry Coe, the listing broker, completely forgot and neglected to market the property. The realtor's "for sale" sign had fallen down on the ground and became overgrown by weeds.

One afternoon in September, as Yeta and Pol were walking around Grand Boulevard, they saw the fallen sign. They walked down to King St. where Coe's office was located.

He called the out-of-town owner, who was a judge in Tempe, Arizona. He was still asking $50,000 because he thought it had already been rezoned into a commercial property. Jerry reminded the judge that, as his agent, he couldn't sell it as a commercial property. His new buyers were buying it as a residential property.

Knowing that the home site was for residential construction, the buyers negotiated the price down to $22,000. They paid cash and closed the sale in a week.

The miniature model house that Pol designed

Meanwhile, Yeta and Pol returned to Florida for the winter months. They kept thinking of the type of house they would build on their oversized home site. They could build a 10,000 square feet house if they wanted to.

The house that Ron Boyce built, based on Pol's design

Pol decided to design a small scale model, which he intended to show to three builders. Then both Pol and Yeta wrote down all the specifications regarding the design and every detail. The house was going to be two stories, with two skylights. They specified that the façade should look like a human face with portholes as eyes, a narrow roof over the entrance as the nose and the main door as mouth.

They wanted three large exposed beams in the living room and a <u>colonial design for a fireplace</u>. They specified a large second floor balcony for a workshop. They also specified a covered decking on two sides of the house. The building would be a country house, with three bedrooms and two bathrooms, with 1750 square feet of living space.

When they returned to Boone in mid-May, they submitted the plans and specification to three builders. The first bid was $180,000 just for the house. The second bid was only $76,000. The third bid didn't arrive until the house was already three quarters finished.

Pol found out why the first bid was so much higher than the second: he was a custom-builder in gated communities. His customers were wealthy businessmen who didn't count their pennies. The second builder was highly recommended by their real estate broker. Ron

Boyes was originally from New Jersey and came up to the mountains to build simple rustic homes for non-pretentious customers.

Fireplace design dates back to colonial times

He was the ideal builder for Yeta and Pol. His workers were all members of the same church. As a group, they had gone to Florida, the Bahamas and the Caribbean Islands to help rebuild the homes of poor victims of hurricanes. This background alone convinced them to give the job to Ron and his crew.

It took the builder only three months to build the house. What they built for the owners was at least ten degrees better than specified, at no extra costs. Those who worked on the house were real artists! They worked with dedication and artistic vision!

Yeta and Pol moved into their new house on August 11, 1991. From the beginning, they were satisfied and happy with their summer home! Yeta was no longer disturbed by the noise because her new home has a lot of mature trees such as white pines, locusts, maples, cherries, birches and dogwoods. There were also many bushes such as azaleas, mountain laurels, rhododendrons and thousands of day lilies. All the plants muffled the noises emitted by trucks, cars, dogs and people.

They turned their condo into a rental apartment and hired a local broker to manage it. They intended to buy more condos when they returned from Florida the following year.

The tin man made from found materials and scraps of wood. Yeta's grandson, Nicky, stood beside the sculpture.

While Ron Boyes was building the house, Pol was constructing his elaborate pathways. The pathways separated into different lines and directions; then, they came together and converged, suggesting to the viewer that they were all connected and somehow united. By then, Pol realized that indeed he was some kind of artist and his primary symbols were pathways. But, he was not the kind of artist who had gone to an art academy. He was not the kind of artist who slavishly followed the artistic traditions that came down from the art masters of yesterday! He was an <u>outsider artist</u> who didn't follow traditions or any rules. He created art as his inner spirit moved him!

He realized that, as an artist, he was primarily a landscaper and his primary symbols were pathways because roads, trails and footpaths signified life itself. He also realized that his philosophy was a form of Taoism. "Tao," in Chinese, meant pathway or life. He thought that pathways were extremely meaningful because everything that humans do must follow a pathway in their minds. Every plan or project is a pathway. Every course, a career or occupation are types of pathways. Religions were also pathways because they provided religious pathways of life. Even the simple act of going to the bathroom at night follows an imaginary pathway.

The Fire Bird in front of the house

The many pathways that Pol built naturally created large and small beds or islands. He turned each bed into distinct gardens, with their own personalities. Every summer, while they lived in Boone, North Carolina, Pol created outdoor sculptures to accentuate each garden. Some of the sculptures were as high as eighteen feet and as wide as ten feet.

It took him about five summers before he felt that he had made enough sculptures and think of another project. He also built a tree house. And, with <u>nineteen Lucy Brock Nursery School children,</u> from age three to four, he created a twelve feet by six feet mosaic artwork on the back of their chimney wall.

The art project with the nursery school children was the most surprising experience for Pol. He was trying to figure out how he could get those little children excited about an art project. First, he designed a Yin-Yang symbol as the focal point. Using strips of mirror, he and Yeta embedded the names of each child on the wall. Seeing their names embedded in the art work made them feel connected to the project and really felt ecstatic!

The Ying-Yang mosaic done with nursery children

Then, Pol asked each child to recycle their old toys. He helped each one install his or her old toys on the wall. This last act of seeing their old toys on the wall convinced them that, indeed, the mosaics were their artwork.

After the wall was finished, the participants had a picnic party at 673 Grand Boulevard, where their art wall stands. Their parents, grandparents, neighbors and friends were present.

Pol had never seen young children so excited about their artwork before. It was hard work but it was worth the effort!

Both of their houses in Cape Coral, Florida, and Boone, North Carolina became tourist magnets. People tend to walk around as if they were in a park. Indeed, the gardens were theme parks because Pol created his pieces to amuse and entertain the children. He has also made things to appeal to the child in everyone.

****

In 1991, Dr. Charles Watkins, the director of the Cultural Museum of the Appalachian State University commissioned Pol to make an appropriate sculpture to be installed in front of the Museum. By August of that year, he installed, "Girtie, the Greeter." In front of the sculpture is a plaque that says, "Pol Mabulbul –From Philosopher to Artist. When Pol Mabulbul taught Philosophy at Philadelphia's Temple University, he had little time for art, but following a second career in real estate and retirement to Florida, his avocation as a sculptor is thriving. His creative efforts first centered around ornamental gardening. Friends frequently commented on how artistic his gardens were and Mabulbul decided to branch into sculpture that incorporated found materials. Mabulbul, born in the Philippines, sees his sculpture as extending from Taoism, a philosophy based upon the idea of following what nature dictates rather than the Western concept of imposing one's will on nature.

"Mabulbul's latest work, **Female Greeter**, will shortly be permanently installed in front of the Appalachian Cultural Museum at University Hall. The ladders that form the woman's arms and legs stand for mobility and people's attempts to succeed, but the ladders are crooked and difficult to climb, suggesting the perils of trying to accomplish anything! Her body, represented by a house, is a symbol of achievement and, in a whimsical note, her belt buckle, made from a potato peeler, points to the entrance of the museum. His garden has become a mecca for tourists and art lovers alike. To them, it's a wonderland but to Mabulbul, philosopher and artist, the garden is simply a natural merging of ultimate principles that govern life and the universe. Charles Alan Watkins, Director of the Appalachian Cultural Museum."

In 1998, Dr. Watkins and Dr. Rao Aluri, the publisher of Parkway Publisher, Inc. commissioned Pol to write a book about his artwork. In April 1999, *My Taoist Vision of Art* came off the press.

Dr. Watkins wrote the Foreword to the book. This is what he wrote about the artist/author: "Art historians ... typically view outsider artists as working through their worldly and personal failures. Pol is a different kind of outsider. His work represents a visual processing of his personal achievements, not simply educational and financial achievements, but those as a human being in balance with the world. In other words, as a Taoist.

"He is, himself, somewhere on a cultural continuum, no longer of the Philippines where he was born and raised, but not so completely American that his vision is colored by over familiarity with the razzamatazz and hurly burly of post-industrial life at the dawn of a new millennium

Dr. Chuck Watkins with Gertie

"... One suspects that if Pol had never started to make art, his gardens would have been based on Eastern principles of simplicity and repose. But he did, in fact, begin to make art and now, rather than simplicity and repose, his gardens have become wonderlands of fantasy and creativity, yet one can still see the Taoist basis that underlies his work. But this is Taoism that has had a head-on collision with Postmodernism.

"When one looks at the garden and the components out of which his art is made---vacuum cleaners, auto gas tanks, tennis racquets, bicycle parts, telephone sets and so forth---the result should be mayhem. But, instead, there is order. In fact, there is more than order. There is a serenity that feels very Eastern, even in the non-orientalness of the setting. The art is not junk sculpture---it is a <u>conscious reordering of the meaning of</u> things, a reforming of artifacts that are moving out of their previous form, much like the journey of Pol from the Philippines to the United States, and into something else. These things---gas tanks and Pol alike---are what they were and what they have become, all at the same time, as if <u>past and present were both visible at once</u>, like an infinity mirror. In the case of the Boone garden, it is a garden of pathways, of wood and branches, ivy, pine needles and pebbles. It is the Orient, and Appalachia, and modern industrialism and the world of handicraft, all merging under some locust and pine trees in the backyard of a most remarkable man!

The Road Roller, made from shopping cart and found objects

"In terms of Appalachian history, this is a good thing. For too long, the general public and many scholars have viewed traditional mountain culture as something eternal, a perpetual Scottish-Irish Nirvana of storytellers and dulcimer players. Mabulbul---the philosopher, artist and gardener---reminds us that no mountain is an island, that change is not only inevitable but healthy and that the view from outside can be quite remarkable."

Chapter Seventeen.
Kiddie Condos

Because of their positive experience with the Daniel Boone condo, Yeta and Pol thought Kiddie Condos would be good investments. Kiddie condos were apartments that rented only to students. They were two bedrooms, two baths that were rented out to four students. By sharing the rent between four people, the apartment became affordable.

Such high density housing became lucrative to landlords because they could charge more rent. In 1991, apartments for students were charging a $1,000 for a 900 square foot unit. It cost each tenant only $250 a month.

All they paid for their unit, at the Daniel Boone condo, was $60,000 in 1986. They estimated that their condo unit was worth at least $70,000 in 1991. They estimated that they could buy "kiddie condos' for no more than $40,000 a unit in 1991.

Consequently, in 1992, they asked their local agent in Boone to shop around for four more condos. They specified two bedroom condos preferably in downtown Boone.

The agent recommended the Kiel-Pat condos on River St. because it was contiguous to the Appalachian State University campus. He said that the units would be easy to rent because the tenants could just walk to their classrooms and they didn't need to own cars. He had also examined the quality of the construction. He personally knew the builder and vouched for his skills and workmanship. He suggested to purchase four of the vacant units at $40,000 a piece.

They applied for a $32,000 mortgage on each unit, amortized at 30 years. Their out-of-pocket investments were only $8,000 for each condo. They instructed their agent to prepare all the condo units for rental as soon as possible and to advertise the condos at $1000 per unit. The agent was able to fill each condo with four college students, without too much problem.

During the first two years of ownership, there was a small positive cash flow. However, by 1995, they suspected that the agent was cheating them. He inflated the cost of repairs especially for the Kiel-

Pat units. The income was barely breaking even. The only positive return of investments was the depreciation of $1200 for each unit, which Pol subtracted from their tax returns. The $1200 depreciation was 15% return of investment, which was not too bad. Still, they had expected better returns of their investments.

If they had managed the condos themselves, they would have a better cash flow. Since they stayed in Boone only six months in a year, they thought that hiring a local manager was the right decision. Moreover, they felt that they didn't understand the rental market in the mountains. For instance, in 1993 they inspected the vacant apartments at Kiel-Pat and found them not in rental condition. Yeta called the agent and registered her opinion about the poor conditions of each unit. But, the agent said that all the units had already been rented. Obviously, the standards of the renters were lower than their own.

Just the same, they were not happy with the kiddie condo investments partly because they distrusted their agent! They instructed the agent to put two condos on the market in 1996. They listed the Kiel-Pat units at $60,000 for each condo. For a whole year, there was no interest; nothing was moving!

Suddenly, during the summer of 1998, Pol opened a letter from a buyer's agent, which said, "I have a buyer who is interested in buying your Daniel Boone Condo. He will pay you $5000 more than your asking price. Please call."

The condo in question was located in the 3rd floor, end unit, of the 1st building on the right

Pol was skeptical because the Boone condo was not listed for sale and because nothing was selling among the Keil-Pat listings. Out of curiosity, he called the buyer's agent. The agent told him that the buyer was serious; that he was a transportation businessman from Charlotte, N.C. He was buying it for his daughter who would be enrolling as a freshman at ASU in the fall semester. He was interested in the Daniel Boone Condo because his agent had told him it was the best unit in the entire Daniel Boone condo development.

Knowing that the buyer was a wealthy buyer made the transaction quick and easy. Since money was no object, the buyer was extremely flexible.

Pol asked his own agent to appraise the Boone condo. In two days, the agent came up with a ball park appraisal of $90,000. He called the buyer's agent and told her, "My asking price is $90,000."

The price was right to the buyer and added his $5000 to the sale price. The condo settled at $95,000, which was the highest price ever paid in the Daniel Boone condominium.

In June 2004, Jim Pruet, the president of the Daniel Boone condo association, told Pol that the same unit would sell for $185,000 or more. The real estate market has been booming in the mountains since 1998.

By 1999, they were able to sell all their units at Kiel-Pat condominium for around $85,000 a unit. To their surprise, they made a little money on each sale. Still, they felt glad to be out of the kiddie condos. They had become aggravations because their agent was making more money from their investments than they did! They also wanted to consolidate their investments in Cape Coral, Florida. They understood real estate investing better in Florida.

Chapter Eighteen.
Undiversified Investments

Critics of real estate investments may point out that the investment scheme of Yeta and Pol was the worst anyone has ever conceived! Number one, it was not diversified!

The first rule of investing, they will point out, is to diversify so as to spread the risk and protect the principal! If all your investments are in one category, like real estate, your chances of success are very poor!

In their defense, the author points out that the principle of diversification makes a lot of sense in the securities market because of the extreme volatility of stock trading! However, their method of investing in real estate was not trading; it was a long term investment. It was owning and managing properties that they could see with their own eyes and touch with their hands. They worked with them, improved them, rented them out to pre-selected clients and reinvested the proceeds in the business. They had complete control of their investments!

It was true, however, that Yeta's and Pol's investments were not sufficiently diversified until December 2004 when they sold five rental houses. By January 2005, they owned a trust fund, four construction loans that yielded between 8% and 12%, several Certificates of Deposits that yielded 6% or better, money market funds and an interest yielding checking account. They still own five rental houses, which provide them enough income to support their lifestyle. This is the type of diversification that they were comfortable with because they controlled their investments, which provided them liquidity!

The other criticism often hurled at real estate ownership is that it is not liquid. What the critics mean is that when the owners try to sell the properties, nobody would buy them. This criticism does not apply to Yeta and Pol either. Real estate is liquid if the seller is prepared to finance the sale. Since the remaining rental houses are at least twenty years old, they have very small indebtedness. Hence, they're ideal candidates for owner financing. Yeta and Pol have already decided that when the time comes to sell them, they would provide the financing if the buyers are not able to obtain their own financing.

Consequently, their scheme of investing is ideal for what they want to achieve---<u>financial independence</u> and <u>freedom from the manipulation of securities brokers.</u>

After they had liquidated five properties, they were looking for new instruments to invest their cash. They attended seminars on estate planning both in Cape Coral, Florida, and in Boone, North Carolina. Both groups of securities brokers they had consulted with advised them to invest in <u>annuities.</u>

When Pol mentioned this experience to his friend, Larry Unterbrink, who for over forty years wrote advisory letters to thousands of securities investors, Larry became a raving madman. "That is the trouble with securities brokers! They are interested only in lining their own pockets with the investor's money! They know that <u>annuities are the worst investments</u> especially for retirees! And, yet, they wine and dine especially seniors and then tell them lies about annuities!

"The real reason why they push annuities is the <u>high</u> <u>commissions</u> involved. They receive 10 to 12 percent in commissions. Since the stock market started going south in 2000, securities brokers have had a hard time making a living just selling stocks.

"When they found out that there were naïve retirees, with money, in Florida and in the Appalachian mountains, that is where some of them went to make a living."

"We nearly bought annuities in Florida because there was supposed to be one type of annuities that was tailored just for retirees," Pol said.

"What made you change your minds?" Larry asked.

"It was the intensity of the broker'sy pursuit! Two brokers visited us at home and they were inviting us to their condo and their yacht club. What made me suspicious was when some big shots were coming down from Orlando just to meet us. We made excuses why we weren't available."

"I'd say you were wise and lucky! There was one thing I forgot to tell you about annuities. It was the <u>small prints</u> that you needed to read carefully. Some of the annuities are not for retirees because some offerings say in small prints that you cannot touch it in 10 or 15 years. If you should withdraw any money before the maturity date, you'll be assessed <u>severe penalties.</u>"

"That is true, Larry. I recently read in the local paper about a 59 year old woman from Wilmington, Delaware. She moved down to Florida with her$269,000 savings. A securities broker advised her to put her money on "equity-indexed annuities." Suddenly, she was reading reports that criticized this type of investments. She read how complex and inappropriate this type of annuities are for seniors. She realized that she bought the wrong instrument of investment. She wants to withdraw her money but it will cost her at least $60,000 in penalties."

"What is she going to do?"

"In order to avoid the severe penalties, she might wait for eight years. She is really angry and she might just withdraw her money, in spite of the penalties!"

"That is a shame! That is why I'm angry at those securities brokers who fleece the seniors of their precious savings."

"Honestly, I had lost confidence in the securities market way back in 1987, when the stock market crashed for no valid reason. Look at how much the average American investors have been duped by unscrupulous brokers."

"For that reason regulators and lawmakers are imposing reforms and penalties. Eliot Spitzer, the crusading New York state attorney general, is demanding from the big brokerage firms that they overhaul their fraudulent stock research. They have been hyping companies that paid them huge investment banking fees!

"At the same time, Congress also passed the Sarbanes-Oxley Act to tighten up accounting and other standards for corporate behavior. With the reforms in place, it appears that Wall Street will become an environment where honest business and honest risk-taking will be encouraged and rewarded!"

"Larry, I'm not buying it. Inside trading is so easy and tempting. Who's going to stop Citigroup or JPMorgan crooks from doing crooked things? Citigroup was fined $275,000 in 2004 for steering customers to invest in Citigroup funds that were unsuitable for them. That penalty was like a slap on the wrist. It didn't even hurt!"

"I'm afraid, I do agree with you Pol."

"You have to agree with me because it was true. For these reasons, I'll continue to keep my distance from the securities market. The big players know how to take care of themselves and how to exploit the weaknesses of the system. A small player like me has no chance in the open marketplace!"

"I have to agree with you again, Pol."

"Larry, I really enjoyed this conversation because you happened to agree with my views on investing. However, you had informed me, in our previous conversation, that you're fully invested in stocks. Obviously, you know so much about stocks that you're comfortable in what you're doing."

"That's true but I keep trying new things, new strategies. Two years ago, I put 40% of my money on one stock because I felt optimistic about the company. I knew that this move was against the principle of diversification. Yet, just last year, I made over $200,000 just on one stock. However, I'm not recommending it to you because the stock may have peaked already!"

"That is fine with me. I'm not ready to return to investing in stocks. I'm still hurting from my losses in 1987. I may never return to investing in the stock market. Yeta is even worse; just the idea of her investments losing value disturbs her! Thanks again, Larry."

"It was nice seeing you again and Yeta. We'll keep in touch. Mary told me that we will have a rendezvous with both of you in Clewiston in about three months."

"Yes, Yeta also told me so. Let us just leave it to the ladies to arrange things to do and see. I'll see you then, in three months. Bye, bye!"

Chapter Nineteen.
Investing in Foreclosures

Some people think that investing in foreclosures is investing in distressed properties. It is true that a lot of distresses are involved in foreclosures. However, much of the distress is often emotional: feelings of guilt, anger, shame and confusion about the future on the part of the debtor who is being foreclosed upon!

There is also a distress in the debtor's financial resources and credit ratings. The person is incapable of properly servicing his mortgage and is threatened with foreclosure. Hence, the villains being portrayed in foreclosure cases are lenders, like banks and private investors who had financed the original sale of a property.

Nevertheless, foreclosures have nothing to do with distressed properties. The circumstances and motives for foreclosure are diverse and complicated. The bad guys are not necessarily the lenders. In fact, there are investors who actually force the lenders to foreclose on properties that are losing value. For instance, Pol's friend, Eddie, bought two home sites on a municipal golf course in Cape Coral, Florida, in 1988. Eddie was speculating that the value of the home sites, right on the municipal golf course, would appreciate considerably within ten years.

Eddie bought a lot for $25,000 and financed it with a $20,000 bank loan. Then, he bought a $30,000 lot and financed it with a $24,000 bank loan. He was speculating as an investor; and the lending bank was also speculating that the properties would appreciate in value and that he would service the loans until maturity or until it was sold.

After ten years had passed, he hired an appraiser to appraise the home sites. His $25,000 investment went down to $12,000 and his $30,000 lot went down to $14,000. Knowing these low appraisals made him decide not to service both loans and forced the bank to foreclose on the home sites. By refusing to service the loans, the bank reluctantly foreclosed on him after three years of procrastination.

He stood to lose $11,000, which were his down payments. But, he stood to save about $600 a month on mortgage fees. In one year, he would have saved $7200. In two years of not making his payments, he would have recouped his losses. From an investment point of view, Eddie felt justified for making the bank take over the financial burden. Since banks normally sell the real estate at a loss, the bank suffered severe loses in these transactions.

Of course, banks don't enjoy being put in such a losing position and punished Eddie by black listing him in the credit community. The bank reported him to the National Credit Bureaus (Experian, Equifax and TransUnion) who promptly informed potential creditors not to extend to Eddie any credit. This retaliatory measure was supposed to hurt Eddie for seven years.

Eddie didn't mind the "red alert" because he had his own sources of financing.

****

The best way to make money on foreclosures is to bid on foreclosed properties at the auction on the steps of the County or City Courthouse. If you do your homework by obtaining a list of foreclosed properties in a given community and paying the services of Title Companies, which check liens and possible clouds on the title, you can make a lot of profit by investing in foreclosures. Realistically, you can make between 20 to 40 percent profit.

On the other hand, if you're not an expert in determining the value of the properties, you also stand to lose a lot of money. You could be paying $100,000 for what is only worth $50,000 or less.

Moreover, you can get into serious legal, economic and nightmarish troubles if you don't know what you're doing.

Since the dawn of the industrial age, people have become specialists in a narrow field for the sake of efficiency, safety and peace of mind. It would be foolish and stupid to deal with literally "everything." Just reflect for a minute, how busy one can be when dealing with "everything." Nobody has enough time or money to deal with so much trivia!

In the same way, there are too many foreclosed properties and there are many phases in the process of foreclosure. It would be wise to choose specific areas and specific phases of foreclosures. In practice, investors have decided to focus on specific phases and values of the process.

For example, some investors have found it easier to deal with the owners before the foreclosure takes place. The advantage of specializing on this phase is that you can examine the property at close range, with all the information from the owners. At this phase, there is little or no competition from the descending horde of competitors!

The investor may treat the transaction as <u>a humanitarian attempt to help out</u> the owner who is in financial trouble. For this reason, you have to decide on the class of persons that you feel you can deal with. Finding such people is a matter of public record. Your city or county will have lists, including the names of people in arrears, the lenders and the addresses of the properties. Sometimes, these types of information are available online. More likely, you have to go to the courthouse and search a computer database or read posted printouts. Or, you can pay $30 or $40 to have the list e-mailed to you by outfits like <u>Foreclosures.com</u> or <u>Foreclosureworld.net</u>.

The next step is to drive to the various addresses and get the <u>curb appeal of the properties</u>. Would you want to own such properties? Do you like the neighborhood? Find out if there are toxic waste dumps nearby. If the property passes a curbside inspection, be ready to pay $300 to $400 for <u>a title search to find out existing liens or claims against the property.</u>

If after the title search, everything still looks good, except for the mortgage lien, then you can <u>negotiate various possible terms with the owner</u>. For example, investor Mike Ballard, of Edmonds, Washington, agreed to assume the $312,000 mortgage of a struggling entrepreneur who was facing foreclosure on his home. The house was appraised at $360,000. Ballard allowed the owner to live in the house for a monthly rent of $1,600. The owner agreed to buy back the house for $390,000 within two years. That would give the investor a profit of $78,000, which is a good profit.

If the owner does not execute his option to buy back the house, Ballard would then sell the house, which was appraised at $425,000. The sale would give him a greater profit of $113,000.

****

The other safer way of investing in foreclosures is to wait until after the auction at the courthouse and buy it through a broker. The discount by then is small; but if the property is in prime location, the long term appreciation will be phenomenal! This was how Yeta and Pol bought their house in Cape Coral, Florida. As described earlier in chapter twelve, they bought their house sight unseen. Through a careful negotiation, they purchased it with a $10,000 discount. The sale was further discounted by another $4,000 by signing the contract within three days. The second discount consisted in the seller's payment of the closing costs.

They bought the Riverfront house for $129,500 in June 1985 from a lending company, which was a subsidiary of General Electric. The lending company had foreclosed on James Walsh few months earlier. The company kept the property because the winning bid at the auction held at the courthouse in Ft. Myers, Florida, was below the indebtedness of the property.

In 1986, they refinanced the house and it was appraised at $350,000. The new appraisal was $220,500 more than they paid for. This higher appraisal was due to some cosmetic renovations that cost them $20,000. They replaced the carpeting with Italian tiles. They replaced the countertops with Briganza Formica and changed the cabinet doors with oak wood. They also covered the swimming pool area with brown river rocks. Much of the appreciation, within a year, was due to the undervaluation done by the listing broker. The broker may have listed the property below market value because he wanted to buy it for his own residence. Such practices obviously happened!

They increased the mortgage on the house to $250,000 and cashed in some of the equity of the house.

In May 2005, they refinanced the house again and it was appraised at $1.2 million. This is another proof that properties in prime areas will appreciate more quickly than other properties in the same community.

****

Here are some pieces of advice especially for neophytes in the foreclosure industry. Buyers at auction have to pay in full and in cash or cashier's check immediately or any time before three P.M. on the day of the auction. If the house is tenanted, the buyer has the responsibility of evicting the occupants.

Buyers at auctions often rehabilitate the property and rent or sell it for at least 20 percent profit. It is wise to do repairs and some cosmetic rehabilitation to improve the curb appeal before selling or renting the property. Doing some cosmetic improvements could increase the <u>profit to 40 percent</u>. Serious investors of foreclosed properties should look for good handy men, who can do small repairs and make some artistic touches. Watch, for instance, the show, "Design to Sell" at House and Gardens on cable TV. Observe the small artistic designs that they make that improve the curb appeal and give greater first impression to the buyer or renter.

As an investor who has made considerable amount of money in rental properties, the author would advise the prospective investors of foreclosed properties to rehabilitate the properties and keep them for rental for a few years. After they have rehabbed the property, refinance the mortgage and allow the property to appreciate for at least ten years. Because it is a leveraged investment, the appreciation will be quick and steady!

Chapter Twenty.
Identity Theft

Yeta had three children by her first marriage. Lorin is a low functioning autistic man. He has been living in a state-run institution, called New Lisbon, in New Jersey. He has a simple job of shredding papers and filling plastic jars with pills in a factory near the institution. He is satisfied with his life because he doesn't know any better and his needs are few and simple! He has no mortgages to service and no fear of being foreclosed upon by some greedy creditor!

Her second child is a woman, whom the author will refer to simply as C. She lived with J in San Diego, Ca. She had a degree in psychology and worked in that field only for a short time. She became proficient in computers and became a hiring specialist in high-tech companies in San Diego.

The third child is Stephanie who teaches in the public school in Philadelphia. She teaches those who are hard of hearing, using the American Sign Language. She is married to a male nurse/English teacher and has two wonderful and beautiful children: a boy and a girl.

****

When the bubble burst in the high-tech companies in 2000, C lost her job and couldn't find a job for two years. J also lost his job in computer staffing and for two years both were languishing economically! Yeta bailed them out of some debts and leased an Infinity SUV in her own name for them to use. She serviced the lease every month.

C defaulted on her mortgage loan and was being foreclosed by a bank. Yeta suggested that they sell the house in San Diego and move to Cape Coral, Florida. They netted at least $400,000 from the sale of the house. They could use the money to start a business in the East Coast.

Both Yeta and Pol suggested that they consider going into real estate investments. Pol pointed out that by using leverage, they could easily buy ten single family homes for rental. They could buy a duplex and live in one unit and rent out the other unit. Due to the use of leverage, ten to eleven units could support their lifestyle. They offered to share their knowledge and expertise to get them started. Their offer was flatly rejected!

Both C and J didn't think real estate was glamorous enough for them! Furthermore, in their ignorant opinion, they said that real estate in Cape Coral was already inflated and had nowhere else to go but down!

Since Yeta and Pol were vacating their Florida house during the summer months, they allowed C and J to live in their house rent free. Yeta paid the use of a phone and the basic utilities.

What they thought was glamorous and had a great potential for great wealth was opening a coffee shop! They had big dreams! They wanted to establish a prototype, which they could duplicate in various communities "a la Starbucks." They decided that Cape Coral wasn't a coffee town. They visited Tallahassee, the capital of Florida, to see if they could establish their prototype there. They also rejected Tallahassee for many reasons. They went to Savanna, Georgia, which they loved very much! However, they foresaw problems with the zoning laws because Savanna was a highly regulated city.

They visited Boone, NC, in September 2002 and bingo! Boone was the ideal place to start their business empire! It so happened that there was a coffee shop on Main St. in Boone that was going out of business. The landlord wanted another coffee shop to reopen there. Appalachian State University was only a block away. The university, with 12,000 students, would provide them with student workers and the students, faculty and administrators would be their logical customers!

By the end of September 2002, they had signed a year lease and were talking to several contractors to completely renovate the store at their high standard of excellence! To impress the coffee world, they removed the old hardwood flooring (oak) that was still in good condition. They ordered cherry wood from California and had it installed. They changed all the fixtures and all the equipments. They upgraded the electrical wirings and the plumbing. They upgraded whatever could be improved for a better curb appeal! They were spending money as if they had millions to spend! They were even bragging to their workers that "money was no object!"

The bragging was stupid because the contractors proceeded to overcharge them for every work rendered. They were from out of town and local contractors were only happy to relieve them of their presumed riches!

****

The first time the author met J, he could immediately tell that he had a very low self esteem! He was naturally bright but suffered from <u>attention deficit</u> <u>syndrome</u>, which caused poor school performance. As a result, he never went to college.

He compensated for his lack of higher education by bragging about his imaginary achievements and non-existent riches! His choices of restaurants were upscale and ordered expensive dishes! He had a penchant for expensive bottles of wine. He indulged himself and his girlfriend with the best that money could buy! At the end of the meals, he picked up the checks, as a rich man should. The only problem was that he had no money! He was spending C's money, which came from the sale of her house.

Wherever they traveled, they stayed in Five Star hotels. For example, when they went to Las Vegas, they stayed in the Belagio, which cost $500 a night. Their favorite hotel was Ritz Carlton where they lodged whenever there was room for them. The most important thing for J was to give the impression of wealth and erudition!

The lack of self-esteem and ADD syndrome would prove destructive to their business right from the start! J decided that he was King of his coffee shop, which he called Jimmy's Java. Because he suffered from ADD, he could not effectively and efficiently work with C. In effect, he alone managed the business. The exclusion of C was a fatal loss because she was pretty, very bright, charming and really personable!

To make matters worse, J believed that as the proprietor, he would regale his customers with his off beat politics. As could be expected, he delighted those who agreed with him. The unfortunate but predictable effect was that he drove away and alienated anyone who disagreed with him!

The biggest damage was caused by ADD. One of the traits suffered by ADD patients was forgetfulness. J often forgot to pay his workers. If he didn't forget to write the checks, just the same, most of the checks bounced! Right from the start, the business was generating a big negative reputation!

****

By the time Yeta and Pol left Boone and returned to Florida in late October, they wondered whether J and C had enough money to finish the renovations.

Knowing that both C and J were prodigals with money, Yeta and Pol had little confidence in their ability to manage a retail business. In the past, J had owned several businesses, which had become bankrupt in a matter of months. In their opinion, C and J were already wasting money. For instance, the old flooring could have been sanded and saved. They didn't have to upgrade the plumbing or the electricity. Those should have been the responsibilities of the landlord.

Just the same, Yeta and Pol wanted to help them out and offered their house in Boone for them to use without paying any rent. The house was only a block away from the coffee shop. Since the phone, electricity and water accounts were in Yeta's name, she insisted that all the bills be sent to her in Florida so that she could pay them. C had a long history of very poor financial management and Yeta was afraid that her own credit reputation might be compromised. Throughout the winter months, Yeta paid the bills, which were C's and J's bills. They had to be careless with their use of electricity in the house because their monthly bills exceeded $500.

****

In the beginning of May 2003, Yeta received two dunning phone calls from American Express. The calls demanded payments for two unpaid accounts. She knew she didn't open the accounts she was being asked to pay and was not worried! She assumed that it was a mistake. By the time they left Florida in mid-May, they had received at least twenty more dunning phone calls from different creditors.

They suspected they were in trouble with unfamiliar creditors but they had no clue as to who caused them! Yeta felt confused and afraid that the "creditors" might put liens on their properties. She was especially concerned about their house in Boone. Since the coffee shop that might have incurred the debts was situated in Boone, she feared that all the liens might be heaped on that property.

However, Pol was convinced that the culprits had to be C and J. They had the motive: to increase their capitalization! He had observed how easily they spent money. He suspected that with their prodigal disposition, they might have run out of money. Yeta, on the other hand, couldn't believe that her own daughter would open several accounts in her name, without her permission!

****

Yeta and Pol left Cape Coral on May 15 and stayed overnight in Richmond Hill, Georgia. They arrived in Boone the next day.

Their first day in Boone was a horrible nightmarish experience! Their phone kept ringing every five minutes, on average, and every ring was a dunning call from some creditor!

They had their phone number disconnected immediately and opened a new <u>unlisted number</u>. Still, some "creditors" got through. Then, creditors of different varieties were sending dunning letters through the regular mail.

Yeta called the three largest national credit agencies: Experian, Equifax and TransUnion and asked them for a copy of their credit report.

The reports confirmed Pol's worst fears! All the three reports showed that several accounts had been opened by J, using Yeta's name, which totaled more than $300,000. They suspected that they had other accounts that had not yet been reported to the credit agencies.

<u>They felt violated, cheated and angry</u>! Pol wanted to go to the police and accuse J and C of identity theft! Yeta, however, couldn't bear the thought of testifying against her own daughter! Yeta might have to do that if Pol had reported them to the police!

They consulted a lawyer who advised them to file an <u>Identity Theft Affidavit</u> that rejected any responsibility for the debts. They didn't authorize those accounts and didn't benefit, in any way, from the merchandises they were presumed to have received. In a notarized document, Yeta swore that "the accounts were opened without my permission or knowledge and without my signature. I do not know the extent of all the accounts that have been opened. I have examined the signatures that I presumably had signed. Those signatures were all forged!"

She visited the local branch of the Centura Bank where C and J had opened a checking account in her name. David T. Jamison, the manager asked her to sign her name on a piece of paper and compared it to the signature on file. Mr. Jamison immediately determined that the signature on file was fraudulent. After a conference with his superiors, Jamison immediately closed the account in their bank.

At Yeta's request, here is a copy of Mr. Jamison's letter to American Express: Yeta felt sure that American Express would believe a bank officer who had personally investigated her case.

J. Adams
Fraud Services
American Express
P.O. Box 297862
Ft. Lauderdale, Fl. 33329-7862

Dear J. Adams:

I am issuing this statement on behalf of Yeta Markowitz in reference to payments made to American Express from an RBC Centura Checking account. Our inquiry into the fraudulent activity experienced by Mrs. Markowitz revealed that her name was added to the business checking account in question against her will and/or without her knowledge and consent. Due to such unsatisfactory activity, the account has been terminated. If you should have further questions, please feel free to contact me at 828-262-4819.

Sincerely,
David T. Jamison
Manager Personal and Business Banking

Unfortunately, the American Express personnel rejected the truth and value of Mr. Jamison's letter because on September 20, 2003, C and J had tricked Yeta to write a check as payment to American Express for $984. They promised to refund her in a couple of days, which they did. Yeta also filed a formal complaint with the <u>Federal Trade Commission</u> and reported the identity theft.

She asked the credit agencies to remove the presumed creditors from her credit reports. However, the agencies refused to comply because those businesses were their own valued primary clients and some of those creditors still insisted that Yeta owed those debts. Consequently, the credit agencies could not afford to displease them. As long as the creditors insisted that an alleged debt was owed, they have no alternative except to report it as a debt. To a certain extent, the credit agencies were nothing more than "debt reporters."

****

<u>C and J had explicitly admitted that they took the liberty to open several accounts in Yeta's name "because we ran out of money."</u> They didn't ask her permission to open the accounts because they felt certain that she wouldn't authorize them.

The theft of Yeta's identity was a clear example of <u>how vulnerable people are to some members of their own families.</u> The identity thieves had access to confidential records and they could easily forge signatures. For these reasons, the creditors are partly to blame for easily granting credits to unknown applicants. Before extending large amounts of credit to unknown borrowers, they should make some routine investigation. For example, they could have contacted Yeta and ascertained whether she had applied for the credits.

The credit system, as it stands, is too lenient in granting credit to almost anyone. Credit cards are frequently issued to persons who did not apply for them. There should be laws against this common practice!

The Federal Trade Commission (FTC) is now aggressively prosecuting criminals and the prosecutors are winning convictions. For instance, in January 2006, a Newburyport, Mass resident was convicted by a US District jury of wire fraud, credit card fraud, conspiracy and aggravated identity theft after a three day trial. The convict used another woman's name and personal information to buy goods and services for five years. She faces up to 32 years in federal prison.

****

In late July 2004, C and J left Boone in the cover of darkness and left their creditors guessing about their destination and new address.

Still the many creditors were determined to collect payments. They promptly turned the debts to <u>collection agencies</u> that were extremely aggressive in trying to collect the debts. The collection agents kept calling Yeta who maintained her position as an identity theft victim.

Her preferred strategy has been to ignore the calls and she keeps an answering machine to record the messages. Still, every now and then, she answers a dunning call especially when she expects calls from friends and relatives.

Instead of feeling defensive, Yeta has taken the <u>offensive</u>! Since Yeta and Pol were prepared to defend themselves in court, she had dared the collectors to take them to court. When no court cases have surfaced after a year of waiting, they assumed that all the <u>dunning calls were desperate attempts to collect uncollectible debts</u>!

In spite of stealing her identity and seriously damaging her credit, C and J had the audacity to ask her in a long formal letter to pay all their debts otherwise the creditors would put liens on her properties. They promised they would pay her "later on." Their promises were empty and untrustworthy! If they were dishonest enough to steal her identity before, they are dishonest enough not to pay her anything in the future. Needless to say, Yeta completely ignored their plea to pay their debts.

What C and J had done to Yeta's credit has been so devastating that no lender would lend her even a dollar today! For example, Wachovia bank, without prior notice, reduced her credit limit on a credit card from $25,000 to $500. She was shopping at Harris Teeter grocery store in Boone, N.C. and had shopped only about $50 worth of merchandise. When she presented her credit card to pay for the merchandise, the store clerk refused it because the bank refused to process it. Yeta was, understandably, shocked and mortified! The embarrassing incident was only a prelude to the abrupt cancellation of her credit card a week later. Her excellent credit history has been destroyed in less than a year. It will take years to repair her credit and financial reputation!

After their house in Florida was badly damaged by Hurricane Charley on August 13, 2004, they applied for a loan from FEMA and the Small Business Bureau. The loan application was summarily denied precisely because of the negative reports from the credit agencies. As a result, they had to pay $110,000 from their own savings for the repair of a failed seawall and a retaining wall. These unexpected expenses seriously strained their financial resources!

****

Pol believes that when C and J left San Diego in 2002, they had already decided to piggy-back their financial fortunes on Yeta's financial status and her sterling credit records. When they were attending a party in Philadelphia in December 2002, J made a remark that shocked Yeta's younger brother, Murray. He said, "C and I intend to steal Pol's and Yeta's identity and will do business in their names." Murray told Yeta about the remark but she interpreted it merely as a joke. Murray didn't think that it was a joke. Quoting Shakespeare, he said, "There was method in his madness."

In retrospect, they did exactly as J had said it at the party. And, they had been planning their criminal strategy for months.

In January 2003, they asked for a copy of Yeta's and Pol's 2002 IRS tax returns. They complied because they were trying to help them in some way. That document alone gave them their social security numbers and other personal information necessary to steal their financial identity. There was no doubt that, unwittingly, they enabled the criminals to steal their identity.

Last June 13, 2002, J incorporated their business, called Jimmy's Java, in the state of Nevada. Without her permission and knowledge, he appointed Yeta as President. He appointed himself as Vice President/General Manager. The incorporation papers proved their illegal intentions way back in June 2002. By making Yeta President, in the incorporation papers, he could then open accounts in her name. He had no qualms about forging her signature.

Neither C nor J has shown any remorse for stealing Yeta's identity. The criminal acts were methodically planned as <u>means to an end</u>. They intended to steal whatever they could in order to sustain the false image of being rich! The affluent image never stuck! Until the last day that they conducted business in Boone and Blowing Rock, North Carolina, the people who knew them only had pity for their miserable lives! Both worked very hard every day but nothing seemed to work! They themselves considered their business efforts as futile and they considered themselves as complete failures! The author sees the causes of their failure to character and personality flaws: 1) extremely low self-esteem and 2) the ADD syndrome. The low self-esteem was caused by the ADD, lack of higher education and lack of a history of achievements in life. To a certain extent, J inherited his father's ADD and suicidal tendencies. His father succeeded in taking his life by using a gun before the age of 40!

****

In January 2005, Yeta decided that she would add a <u>little humor</u> to the dunning phone conversation. Since she had consistently claimed to be an identity theft victim, she couldn't logically talk to the callers as if she owed the caller any money.

Every time someone asked for her, she made up an imaginary story about where she was and what she was doing. Among her stories was that Yeta was traveling around the world spending stolen money. Sometimes, she said, "Yeta is out robbing a bank." However, her favorite story was, "Yeta is now living in the Philippines." When asked for her phone in that country, she responded, "They don't use phones in that country."

"Is that true?"

"Oh, yes!"

****

One day, a woman asked for Yeta. "She is not in; she is in the Himalayas preparing to climb Mt. Everest."

"How old is she?"
"She is only 97 going on 57. She is athletic and adventurous."
"Are you pulling my leg?"
"Yes!"

****

At another time, an aggressive man asked for Yeta. "She is away in the Colorado River, rafting in the rapids!"
"Are you serious?"
"No! It's none of your business!"

****

Ironically, her facetious responses had taken the wind out of the caller's sails. They could tell that she wasn't taking them seriously. They were getting her message, which was, "Don't bother me. I'm not the person who owed you the money. I'm an identity theft victim!"

Interestingly, as of July 2005, the dunning phone calls just stopped! The debt collectors have reached the conclusion that they were not going to collect anything from her. Yeta has finally outsmarted them and now she can finally answer her phone calls without feeling defensive and anxious! This has been a great relief!

****

Reader, your identity too can be easily stolen and some crooks may even sell it on the Internet chat rooms. Each year, 7 to 10 million Americans become victims of identity theft. The majority of them don't know the thieves personally. From the massive data-brokerage firms, to your local banks, your identity is available to the average crook! There are even "chat rooms" on the Internet where the ID thieves buy and sell financial information, social security numbers and, of course, someone's ID.

The lead article in the recent Money Magazine issue was, "Toddler Fraud,"(December 2005). The writer estimated that 4% of the victims are infants and very young children. The perpetrators are relatives, including parents. Those innocent victims have no idea that when they are old enough to apply for credit, no one will extend it to him or her because some adult relatives had perpetrated the crime when they were just babies. As soon as a Social Security Number had been filed for a child, that baby is already vulnerable to ID theft!

Here are the common sources of information for the ID thieves. Your banks, school, employer, doctor, Federal agencies, phone companies, payment processing agencies, data-brokerage firms, credit-reference agencies, card networks and ordinary merchants.

ID thieves today use both low- and high-technology to get the necessary information. Here are some of the popular tactics. The first one is <u>dumpster diving</u> where the thief rifles through the trash bins for loan applications, credit-card documents and any printed Social Security numbers.

There is a strange term called, <u>phishing</u>, in which the crooks pose by e-mailing you or phoning you and posing as a legitimate company and claiming that there is a problem with your account. The phony "problem" becomes the excuse to extract confidential information. If you make the mistake of believing the crook and you provide him your confidential information, your identity is stolen!

There is another trick called, <u>skimming</u>, in which the crook steals credit or debit-card numbers by attaching a data-storage device to an ATM machine or attaching a card reader to a retail checkout terminal.

Then, there is <u>shoulder surfing</u> in which the thief lurks at ATM machines or phone booths to pick off PINs, credit-card numbers or passwords. If you notice someone hanging around close to an ATM machine, leave and use another machine where no "surfer" is hanging around.

****

There are many recent examples of accounts that had been compromised for different stupid reasons. In April 2004, a shoe chain called, DSW, revealed that hackers had stolen data from 1.4 million credit-and debit-cards transactions at 108 stores in 25 states. The breach also included account numbers from 96,000 check transactions.

The processing agency, Card Systems, improperly retained information on credit card customers for research. When hackers hit its system in May 2004, it exposed 40 million customers to potential identity thieves.

Bank of America and Wachovia Bank worked with upper-level employees in April 2004 to identify vital customer information. A middle man sold 676,000 account numbers to outsiders.

In 2004, Choice Point, a processing agency sent 145,000 reports of stocks with the names, Social Security numbers and financial information to "phishing" con men who posed as legitimate debt-collectors for an insurance and check-cashing businesses.

In May 2004, UPS picked up a parcel of tapes from CitiFinancial addressed somewhere in the state of Texas. The parcel contained 3.9 million customer's addresses, Social Security numbers and loan-payment records in New Jersey. The parcel never arrived at its Texas destination. As of August 2005, nobody knew where the parcel was.

On March 11, 2005, a Berkeley graduate student's laptop computer was stolen. The theft exposed 98,400 graduate students and applicants to ID thieves. The computer had the students' names and Social Security numbers. The Social Security number gives the thieves the key to open up all kinds of accounts that the thieves could use.

Also in March 2005, backup tapes containing nearly 20 years worth of Time Warner's 600,000 employee's names and matching Social Security numbers went missing from the back of a Ford Econoline van, while being hauled to a storage by Iron Mountain, a leading off-site data-protection firm. None of the information was protected because the data were not encrypted.

On April 5, 2005, an MCI laptop filled with sensitive personal information of 16,500 current and former MCI employees was stolen from a staffer's car. The vehicle was not locked.

These are scary everyday events that should make you realize that you are not safe from ID thieves!

****

The information that ID thieves want from you are credit-card numbers, CW2 security numbers (found on the back of the credit card), credit reports, Social Security numbers, ATM cards, telephone calling cards, mortgage details, date of birth, passwords/PINs, home addresses and phone numbers.

Protect yourself by photocopying all credit-cards, investment and bank account information. Always keep your credit card receipts; you will need them when you file reports to the police or to the Federal Trade Commission (FTC). Place a preemptive fraud alert on all credit reports. What this means is when someone tries to open a credit in your name, the issuing company calls the credit card agencies (Experion, TransUnion and Equifax) to check if you had applied for the credit. The credit card agency will, then, call you to ascertain whether you did apply. If you didn't apply, the issuer would then refuse the application and probably inform the police.

If you find out that you are an identity theft victim, place a fraud alert on your credit report by calling Experian (phone 888-EXPERIAN) or Equifax (888-766-0008) or TransUnion (800-680-7289). You don't have to call each agency. When you contact one of the agencies, that agency will inform the others.

Review the reports carefully to isolate unsolicited inquiries about your credit; check unknown accounts and debts. Get the agencies to remove the accounts that are not yours.

Close all the accounts that are not yours. Follow up in writing with copies of supporting documents. Choose new password for new accounts. For fraudulent charges on existing accounts, fill out a fraud-dispute form. For new unauthorized accounts, submit the FTC's ID Theft affidavit.

The next step is to report to the local police or to the police where your ID was stolen. Get a copy of the police report because creditors will require a copy of the report to establish your credibility. Finally, file a complaint with the Federal Trade Commission. This will further establish your credibility.

The reader may wonder how the ID thieves, who now possess the private information and the identities of millions, turn them into cash or valuable merchandise? Download some of the chat rooms on the Internets where crooks are directly selling stolen identities for as little as $5.00. There is a possibility that your own identity is up for sale!

In January 2005, a USA Today staff spent five months tracking down some of the victims of cyber fraud. In cooperation with law enforcement officials, tech security experts and Internet underground operatives, they documented the stories of three victims. Last July 11, 2005, they published their report entitled, "Cybercrooks Lure Citizens Into International Crime," by Byron Acohido and Jon Swartz. The real names of the victims have been changed for their physical safety and anonymity.

The case of Karl, a 38-year-old former cabdriver started on April 5, 2005. In his local paper, *The Union* in Grass Valley, California, he read this advertisement, "Look at this! WORK AT HOME! Correspondence manager vacancies. MAIL PACKAGES from home without leaving your job. Easy! Ship parcels from our clients. Get paid $24 per parcel! Info: http://kflogistics.biz/vacancies.asp.htm."

The ad beckoned to him like a life preserver. The prospect of getting paid just for shipping packages from home in his spare time seemed godsend. He assumed that the ad was legitimate since it appeared in his own local paper, which had a good reputation.

He applied for the job and was immediately accepted. He received an e-mail, which informed him that he would receive packages of digital cameras and laptop computers from online merchants. The e-mail instructed him to repackage the merchandise, apply the addresses that would be sent to him and then send the package to Russia.

Because Karl kept all the e-mails, letters, credit card statements, packing receipts and mailing labels, USA Today was able to put together the exact sequence of his first transactions.

April 18, 2005. Someone from a bogus website at the center of the scam, kflogistics.biz, tested a $1 charge on iWon.com, a prize-giveaway Web page, using a Bank One Visa credit card number stolen from Brian Spoutz, a 48-year-old San Jose, Calif., soft-ware salesman. (A Visa investigator later notified him about the compromised card in May 2005.)

April 20. Kflogistics.biz used Spoutz Visa card to place an order at Newegg.com for $2,607 digital camera and extra memory. It directed shipment of two separate parcels to a home in Gilroy, Calif.

April 22. FedEx attempted to deliver the parcels but the reshipper in Gilroy had developed cold feet and was not home. Using FedEx online tracking, Michael Birman, of kflogistics.biz, noted the failed delivery. He contacted FedEx and redirected the delivery to Karl in Grass Valley, Calif. Birman alerted Karl via e-mail about the two parcels.

April 23. Birman contacted UPS.com. Using a hot credit card number, he purchased $48 Global Express Mail shipping label addressed to Roman Radeckiv in Moscow. Then, he downloaded the new label as a JPEG image file. He attached the file to an e-mail to Karl. He instructed Karl to combine the two parcels.

April 24. FedEx delivered the two parcels to Karl in Grass Valley.

April 27. Karl printed out the JPEG label. He repacked the camera and memory into one box. He affixed the printed label and completed the shipment. Karl observed, "The operation was amazing. It was highly coordinated."

Within weeks, Karl had sent off six packages. Little did he suspect that he had become an unwitting recruit in a growing scheme to assist online criminals. This latest phenomenon in digital fraud costs American e-merchants millions of dollars a year.

People like Karl are called "mules" because they haul the dirty work for the crooks, who operate outside the United States. Shortly after he sent the parcel to Moscow, he noticed a $4,358 electronic deposit in his online bank account. Birman instructed him to deduct a small amount for his troubles but to wire the rest of the money to Moscow.

Suddenly, he became suspicious and afraid that he was embroiled in a crime operation and went to the authorities. As a result, his bank froze the $4,358 money. Thereafter, he received calls from several people who threatened to harm him. One man asked him when he was going to be home. He became seriously concerned about his physical safety!

Then, he unexpectedly received account statements intended for online banking customers from across the United States. Some unknown crook had changed the billing addresses of stolen credit cards and bank account numbers to his residence. He was getting extremely deep in trouble!

One of the letters was intended for a 28-year-old Ryan Sesker of Des Moines, Iowa. Chase bank was granting his request to increase his credit limit from $3500 to $5000. The big trouble was that Ryan never made the request. Some online criminal made the request in order to draw $4,300 from Sesker's account.

Mules, like Karl, served two functions for the crooks: they kept the goods flowing through a tightly run distribution system and they insulated the criminals from the police. When the police followed the trails of counterfeit merchandise, the people they apprehended were the mules, not the criminals that they wanted.

With the help of law enforcement officials, postal inspectors and computer security experts, USA Today identified 21 reshipping operations, with polished websites and slick online job application programs. They advertised on popular employment websites such as Monster.com, CareerBuilder.com and Jobfinder.com.

Their targeted mules were people who were unemployed, under-employed and retirees who could not afford their retirement. Among the recently recruited mules was Irene Rodriguez, 38, who was a longtime bulk-mail handler from San Jose, California. She was looking for an extra income to finance her daughter's senior prom gown. Last February 2005, she applied for a job that promised to pay her $30 to $50 per shipment. She read about the job from CareerBuilder.com and assumed that it was legitimate.

About the same time, Lynn Malito, 46, a single mother of two, got laid off from her job as a dispatcher for a trucking company in Memphis, Tennessee. She responded to the ad on Monster.com to reship packages for CNetExpress.

Karl, Rodriguez and Malito ended up as shipping mules but abruptly quit their jobs and reported their experiences to the police when they became suspicious about the criminal nature of the shipments. "I was petrified," Malito said. "I thought I was going down, getting arrested for my role in this crooked business."

Because there was no criminal intent on their part, they would not be prosecuted. Federal prosecutors have dismissed a number of mules they had tract down because they didn't know what they were going into.

****

Some seniors, with cash flow problems, have been duped into similar scams, with a different twist. Some bogus companies advertised with high powered names like, Xian Energy, Delta Soft Labs, International Health Care, Future Tech, V-Tech Sendit Software, etc. and promised considerable payment for little effort. But, the only rewards they got were depleted bank accounts.

The "big companies" were supposed to be based overseas and were recruiting "work at home representatives" through e-mails and online job postings. They claimed that "due to the delays in clearing checks and money orders in Europe, they needed financial agents to process payments for their U.S. orders." The recruited mules were promised to receive checks between $2,000 and $100,000 via FedEx. After depositing the checks in their own accounts, all they had to do was wire-transfer those funds to a foreign bank. After the checks had cleared, they would then receive a five percent commission.

Dick Hambrice, 67, a retired medical supplies salesman from Columbus, Ga. said, "Since I live on Social Security, an additional $200 or $300 a week would really be helpful." Instead, he lost $4,500 because the check he received was counterfeit. So, the money he sent to a foreign bank was actually his own.

This type of check-cashing scheme generates complaints each month to the Internet Crime Complaint Center. It is one of the most common Internet scams. To add insult to the injury, the victim may face federal counterfeiting and forgery charges for signing or processing bogus checks.

The lesson here is to be very wary of "work at home offers," especially those with foreign connections. The foreign connection makes the prosecution of the fraud impossible to pursue.

If someone sends you money and wants the money wired back to a foreign address, it is a scam! Treat the offer like a deadly plague!

Check your bank account every day, if you can, and examine whether the charges and debits are legitimate. Check the deposits too. If you notice irregularities, contact one of the credit agencies

(Equifax, Experian or TransUnion) and block further fraudulent transactions!

To make it easier to check your bank account every day, open an account on the Internet. With such an account, you can check your account every day or every hour, as you please!

****

On July 29, 2005, Equifax, one of the nationwide consumer reporting companies, sent Yeta a report that many of the former creditors in her file had been removed. Suddenly, the creditors that had sullied her credit and economic reputation, due to identity theft, had stopped making the same report. This meant that they finally believed her that she was a victim of identity theft.

Creditors, however, are generally sore losers! There were very few "creditors" who admitted errors and asked for apology.

What creditors normally do is to follow the *standard procedures*. If a presumed debt had not been paid after 180 days or more, they send it to collection agencies, which use intimidation, harassment, threats and unheard of illegal tactics. For a high percentage portion of the debt, collection agencies hire thugs and criminal elements to shake down the presumed debtors. The amount of intimidation and verbal abuse they inflict on presumed debtors are highly obscene and illegal!

After about a year of trying to obtain payment by using questionable means, the creditors would then move to the next step, which is to foreclose, if there is any collateral to the debt. Or, the creditors may negotiate for a voluntary surrender of the collateral. In cases of cars, vans, RVs, etc., they authorize mandatory repossession.

By the end of a fiscal year, if the debt is still not paid, the creditors may instruct their accountants to charge off the debt as a tax deduction. After this tax event, it doesn't matter to the creditor why the debt was not paid. In the end, the unpaid debt does not cost the creditor any money. Writing off a debt as a tax loss costs the tax payers, not the business creditors. This explains why many credit card lenders are irresponsible in extending credits even to minors and to people with questionable reputation. They know that they won't really lose any money.

Moreover, the creditors do not care whether the harassments and endless abuse of the identity theft victims were justified or not. It is up to the victims to heal their emotional and financial wounds!

In fairness to the identity theft victims, creditors should explicitly help the victims by positively clearing their names and restoring their good credit ratings. The author expects to see greater fairness in the future if <u>laws restricting credit to crooks are passed</u>. Collection agents should be prohibited from using harassment techniques that inflict emotional pain! It is a good business practice for creditors to mend their relationships with consumers who had patronized their companies for many years.

For instance, American Express has alienated Yeta for not believing her claim of being an ID theft victim. She was a loyal customer of the company for over forty years. Unless the company makes the proper apology, she will continue to distance herself from it and withhold her pa tronage.

****

On September 20, 2005, TransUnion wrote to Yeta, "If our investigation has not resolved your dispute, you may add a 100-word statement to your report."

On September 29, 2005, Yeta sent the following statement, "I am requesting that the following statement be added to my credit report on the advice of the Federal Trade Commission.

"I am an Identity Theft Victim. The following companies have refused to cooperate even though I have submitted all documents requested including police reports and my affidavit verifying that my signature was forged, etc. The disputed accounts are American Express, Dell, Nissan and Mecklenburg Superior Court. I did not open these accounts or received any merchandise or services from these accounts.

"There are 40 accounts marked paid or paying as agreed. These are my current accounts. There are still 4 disputed accounts.

"Sincerely, Yeta Markowitz"

The author didn't realize how important a good credit was in any investment venture. Before Yeta became an ID victim, she received all kinds of offers every month of <u>pre-approved credit cards</u> to increase her buying power and her investment potentials. After her identity had been stolen, all the offers dried up! Fortunately, she is at the stage of her life when she no longer needs new credit!

She carries only one <u>secured credit card</u> for the sake of convenience. There are some business transactions where cash does not work; car rental is among them. A "secured credit card" means that she had deposited a certain amount of money with a bank. The deposit earns a good interest and she can use her credit card only up to the amount of her deposit. As of April 10, her birthday, she has adjusted to her new status and limited circumstances. To four remaining creditors, she is still labeled "a deadbeat!" These, too, shall pass!

Chapter Twenty One.
Hurricanes and Tornadoes of Florida

The hurricanes and the tornadoes that hurricanes generate seriously threaten real estate investments especially in Florida! Every storm season, landlords in Florida shiver in fear that their investments might be submerged by storm surges or blown away by hurricane force winds or F-5 tornadoes! Having insurance allays some of the fear! Unfortunately, the hurricane damage deductible is 5% of the value of the property. In 2004, the actual amount of the deduction for their home in Cape Coral was $9,500, which was high but still fair! Due to this high deductible, Yeta and Pol couldn't collect anything to cover the cost of the damage to their seawall and retaining wall!

The hurricane and tornado devastation of Florida properties during the summer of 2004 and the inundation caused by Hurricane Katrina in the summer of 2005 have taught investors some sobering lessons! You can have flood and wind insurance and sustain flood and wind damages that cost you over $100,000 to repair or restore but get nothing from your insurance carrier or from the government. This was what Yeta and Pol experienced in Cape Coral on August 13, 2004. <u>Their insurance coverage excluded seawalls, retaining walls and docks.</u>

Ironically, many victims of Katrina, who <u>lost their homes through flooding in the Gulf Coast, may get nothing</u> because they had no flood insurance. Somehow, the owners had assumed that they were not in a flood zone!

The potential for catastrophic losses in hurricanes and tornadoes are unpredictable and incalculable! Owning properties in coastal regions and flood prone areas is a big gamble for any investor!

Real estate investors take a calculated risk by owning investment properties along the storm pathways! Consider, for example, the plight of real estate investors who lost their properties along the Gulf Coast when Hurricane Katrina devastated the area. Suddenly, they lost their tenants who became homeless and lost rental revenues since their tenants won't be sending their rent money for months or years to come! Furthermore, they'll <u>continue paying mortgages for rental properties that no longer exist</u>. It could mean bankruptcy for some investors!

Nevertheless, the hurricanes in Florida are part of the exciting but risky life in the tropics! Every year, from the beginning of June to the end of November, storms that form somewhere in the tropics, arrive naturally in the Gulf of Mexico or the east coast of Florida, like the predictable rising sun! It is nature's way of adjusting the atmospheric imbalances that occur especially in the tropics. The imbalances are caused by different factors in the ocean, such as the ocean currents, the water temperature and the salinity of the water.

Imbalances are also caused by changes of magnetic forces on magnetic fields on the surface of the earth. Furthermore, the basic rotation of the earth on its axis causes forces and winds to shift and move in unpredictable ways!

Storms also occur because of high humidity and wind in the atmosphere. Humid air releases rain as it rises off the ocean. As air rises, more air and wind are sucked in to replace the rising elements. The earth's rotation influences the inward flow of winds so that they make a circular motion. The spinning storms create bands that spiral around an eye wall. The storm grows as more warm and moist airs are drawn in. Moist air rises through the storm bands, which produce a lot of rain.

Winds spiral in tighter and faster circles as they approach the storm's center. The eye wall is the most devastating part of the storm. The eye looks hollow because the air sinks through the center, leaving the area clear and cloudless.

****

The North and the South Poles are the pivotal points of the <u>ocean currents.</u>

Starting from about 400 miles from the Antarctic Pole, the Antarctic current naturally moves towards the Arctic Pole. About 400 miles from the Arctic Pole, the current sinks down and reverses its course to the south. Hence, there is a continuous flow of <u>conveyor-like currents in the oceans</u>. The temperature and salinity of the currents are continually changing, depending on the changes occurring in the Poles.

Recently, since the end of the cold war, international scientists have jointly studied both Poles. They have discovered some critical changes happening at the <u>Arctic Polar cap</u>. The ice cap, that acts as insulator and prevents the heat from escaping from that part of the earth, has thinned out. This means that the arctic seal has been broken and a lot of heat is coming out of the North Pole! In fact, the aurora borealis of the Northern Hemisphere is probably part of the heat that escapes from the polar cap.

The scientists have estimated that the ice loss in the ice cap has been 50% just during the last 30 years! In some areas of northern Alaska, <u>the permafrost has been melting and the terrain has been pockmarked</u>. The melting ice has caused houses to sink; some trees have fallen to the ground because the supporting soil has softened. Some Arctic animals have been isolated geographically from their normal habitats. Some scientists now predict that the polar bears might become extinct!

This warming trend means that the ocean currents, which return towards the equator have been warmer especially during the summer months. The hotter water temperatures may be causing the new cycle of storms in the tropics. Last summer of 2004, when four major hurricanes formed in the tropics, some scientists have estimated that the ocean temperature was only about one degree higher than normal. How many more major storms will form if the ocean water were 4 or 5 degrees higher? There could be ten times more hurricanes when that happens!

<u>Global warming</u> is not a theory; it is a <u>fact</u>! <u>The melting of the permafrost has been studied extensively and documented</u> by <u>International Scientists</u>. The increasing levels of the ocean waters brought about by the melting glaziers have been carefully measured in Bangladesh and in the low lying islands in the Pacific.

In 2004, "killer heat waves" scorched France and Italy. In 2005, heat waves have devastated especially the southwest USA and Chicago. Extreme heat readings of 125 degrees have been measured in certain places in California. The thermometer reading in Las Vegas was 117 degrees for several days. As of July 26, 2005, at least forty people have died from the heatwave, most of the casualties were elderly.

Fortunately, the Antarctic icecap had grown thicker. The scientists have been drilling on the ice to study the compositions of different layers. They have drilled down to 3,000 feet and are learning a lot of interesting data about the earth and the climatological conditions and changes that have occurred there over time.

Yeta and Pol have lived in southwest Florida for over twenty years but they experienced their first hurricane only during August 2004. Hurricane Charley passed through their safe haven with a vengeance!

Pol has cursorily studied the Florida hurricanes since they relocated in Florida in July 1985. By 1987, he had concluded that the southwest section of the state was the safest place to be in the state of Florida! Every year, he tracked the pathways of each storm as a hobby.

He concluded that storms formed either in the Gulf of Mexico, or west of Africa or in the southern Atlantic Ocean. If a storm formed in the Gulf, the predictable movement of the storm was to go northwest due to the influence of the trade winds, which normally blow from the northeast in the northern hemisphere. There is a high probability that the storms in the Gulf would move in that direction. Hence, the storm landfall could be Texas, Louisiana, Mississippi, Alabama or the Panhandle of Florida.

If a storm started in the Bahamas, normally it would move northwards and dissipate in the north Atlantic. Sometimes, a Bahamian storm also went towards the northwest and landed in New York or the New England States.

There have been few storms in the Bahamas that moved directly westward and hit the east coast of Florida. Among the few occurred in August 1992. Hurricane Andrew formed in the Bahamas and pulverized Homestead, Florida as a category 5 storm. It crossed the state and exited to the Gulf of Mexico and crossed the Gulf waters to devastate Louisiana as a category 2 hurricane! Andrew left a catastrophic destruction both in Florida and in Louisiana that exceeded $34 billions!

Another devastating storm from the Bahamas that hit North Miami in late August 2005 was Hurricane Katrina. She hit as a category one hurricane and killed eleven people! Her more devastating landfall was in the Gulf Coast as a category 4 hurricane! Her storm surge was 29 feet and created perhaps the worst damage in history!

However, the storms that continually threatened Florida originated from West Africa, which moved westward through the Caribbean Islands. As they moved towards the northwest, they followed a path directly towards the Gulf of Mexico.

A storm pathway is a relatively open body of water that gives the least resistance to strong winds and rain. As soon as a storm had entered the Gulf, it usually continued to move towards the northwest, unless another weather system, like a trough or a depression coming from the northwest, forced it to move further east, towards the Florida Panhandle.

Southwest Florida had been safe from the storms since 1960 when Hurricane "Donna" made a landfall in Ft. Myers. Consequently, it had been forty three years ago when a category 4 hurricane devastated the area.

The way the storms formed in the tropics, during the summer of 2004, made that season exceptional! Category 4 Hurricane Charley made a landfall on August 13 2004 and eviscerated Port Charlotte and Punta Gorda.

On September 5, a bigger hurricane had formed in the Bahamas. Hurricane "Frances" was as big as the state of Texas, although it was only a category 2 storm. Because it was a slow moving storm, it dumped at least 20 inches of rain in the East Coast of the Florida! It forced 2.8 million people to flee their homes and left nearly 5 million people without electric power. Frances would cost the state between $2 billion to $10 billion.

Even though Frances had been downgraded to category 2, it still packed a lot of punch especially on its north side. The National Hurricane Center reported gusts of winds that measured 124 miles per hour. The eye of the storm made a landfall at Sewall's Point, just east of Stuart, at 1 A.M. Sunday, September 6. The top sustained winds were recorded at 105 mph.

"Normal life" suddenly became insomnia, power outages, compulsory evacuation orders, gas rationing, fear and fatigue! All around were millions of cubic yards of broken tree limbs, corrugated metals, twisted aluminum sidings and many other categories of debris.

Hurricane Frances was still ravaging the state of Florida when another killer storm was forming in the Caribbean islands! All attention quickly shifted to a new storm, called "Ivan," who, in 16 hours, quickly developed from category 1 to 4, packing winds of 135 mph, moving west-northwest at 21 mph. Ivan was located approximately 760 miles east-southeast of Barbados.

On September 7, Ivan became a category 5 with winds of 160 mph and devastated the island of Grenada! It also destroyed the western portion of Jamaica. Ivan's predicted landfall was Gulf Shores, Alabama.

"Everyone is on their last good nerves," said Steve Albrecht, administrator of the Riverside Behavioral Center, a Ft. Myers local hospital. "Things that normally wouldn't bother you are sending people over the edge! Even if Ivan blows past us, there's going to be huge psychological reactions that we're going to be seeing for many months and even years to come."

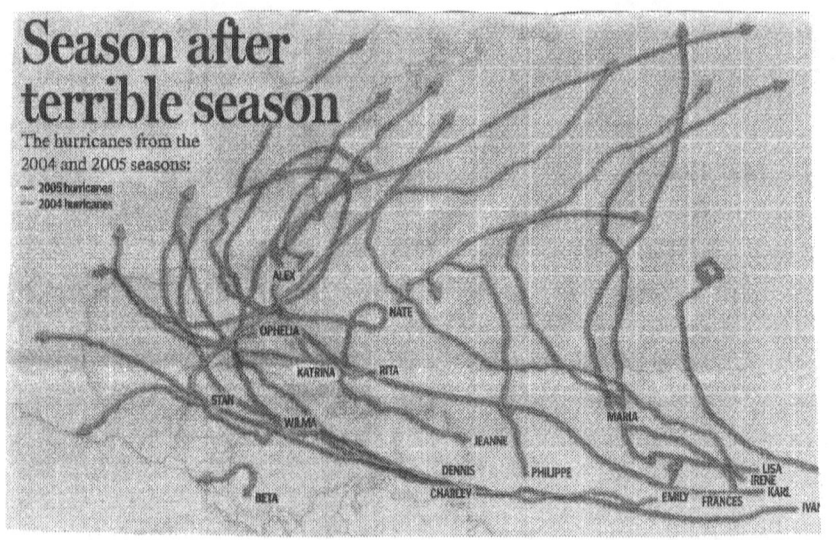

Season after terrible season

The hurricanes from the 2004 and 2005 seasons:

— 2005 hurricanes
— 2004 hurricanes

Cindy Way, 46, a mental health counselor in Punta Gorda said, "People have had their feeling of security shaken by the first storm, Charley. Shelter, food, your ability to get water, your ability to communicate with other people---those are basic needs. And, when you've lost that or seen it lost, it's extreme fear that follows! Without those things, you can die!"

As a by-stander also observed, "Ivan is interrupting an already tattered routine. Everyone is an emotional wreck!"

Another woman also added an opinion, "I'm nervous, anxious and crying without obvious reasons. My mental health is kind of like: 'if I wake up tomorrow, fine. If I don't, that's ok too'."

Even though Ivan was redundant and not relevant any more to people's lives, the hurricane still made a landfall on September 16 in Gulf Shores, Alabama, just west of Pensacola, Florida. Ivan, as a category 3 hurricane, caused considerable damage to properties and killed 23 people.

As if three hurricanes were not enough, Hurricane "Jeanne" also formed in the Caribbean islands. She killed 1,500 people in Haiti and badly devastated the island. On September 25, she made a landfall exactly where Hurricane Frances had made a landfall. By the time the four hurricanes had gone off to sea, the damage to properties was estimated at $42 billions, which surpassed the $34.9 billion damage caused by Andrew in Florida and in Louisiana in 1992. There were 117 people killed. More than 25,000 homes were destroyed and 4,600 homes sustained major damage!

****

Yeta and Pol experienced the wrath of Charley only incidentally. Normally, they lived safely in Boone, NC during the summer months.

On the 10th of August 2004, however, they had to return to Cape Coral for an unfinished business. They had listed three rental houses for sale. On the 12th of August, they watched on television how Charley eviscerated the island of Cuba with 145 mph winds! The next day, the 13th, they watched nervously as Charley was upgraded to category 4. They allayed their fear with the forecast that the hurricane would hit Tampa/St. Petersburg. That predicted landfall was at least 80 miles north of Cape Coral.

The seawall damage was more serious than Yeta and Pol had suspected. When Reagan examined the damage more carefully, he found out that the entire seawall, needed to be replaced. The sections of the wall that had fallen down were caused by the rusting of the iron tie-rods that kept them in place. The old technology just used unprotected iron, which rusted in less than ten years. He would have to replace the remaining seawall and use epoxy-coated iron rods, which should last for at least a hundred years. He would tie them up to eight concrete posts, called "dead men" (situated ten feet away on land).

The workmen would also remove the existing art wall (a 5 foot by 80 foot retaining wall covered with mosaics). They would construct a new retaining wall at the second level, above the seawall, but with a fifteen foot set back. The total cost, including a new land fill and landscaping, was $110,000. This portion of the property could not be insured, not even by the government; hence the money had to come from their savings.

The partly destroyed art wall by Hurricane Charley

****

Based on the storm activities during the months of June and July 2005, there were good reasons to be concerned about the 2005 storm season! Storms Cindy and Dennis hit the state of Florida in less than a week from each other, during the month of July. On July 8, Hurricane Dennis had been upgraded to category 4 and packed a wind force of 150 miles per hour as it made a landfall in Cuba! It was expected to become a category 5 before it hit the Florida peninsula! Dennis was a vast and devastating hurricane!

It was only the third week of July and the fifth hurricane of the season, named Emily, also formed in the Caribbean islands! She entered the Gulf of Mexico and proceeded to hammer the Yucatan peninsula of eastern Mexico. After the Yucatan peninsula, Emily proceeded to destroy northern Mexico, just south of Texas! In the early morning of July 20, 2005, Emily was upgraded to category 3 and the eye of the storm slammed into land just south of Brownsville, Texas at 120 mph! Northern Mexico bore the major brunt of Emily!

In early August, the National Weather Service revised its hurricane prediction upwards for the 2005 season from 15 to 21! At the same time, Professor William Gray of Colorado State University also revised his predictions upwards: from 15 to 20 storms for 2005! What was alarming about both predictions was that this was the highest seasonal forecast of hurricane activity ever made since Professor Gray started forecasting in 1984! Gray said, "Based on research data obtained through July, we <u>foresee one of the most active hurricane seasons on record!</u>"

As of August 10, 2005, the season had an unprecedented number of storms with eight storms, including two hurricanes, making landfalls in Florida! Gray predicted that 10 hurricanes, six of which would be severe, would hit the eastern seaboard of the United States in 2005!

The dire predictions were based on the following data: ocean warming in the tropics, low tropical sea pressure, increased rainfall in West Africa, a large mass of very dry air originating from the African continent and the lack of El Nino conditions in the Pacific Ocean.

The National Weather Service pointed out, in its Web site, that "the devastating 2004 hurricane season was not an aberration. In fact, such active seasons are likely to be the norm for the next 15 to 30 years. While the total number of storms making landfall may vary, the <u>total number of major hurricanes that develop is expected to remain above average during the 2005 season…</u>."

The National Weather Service also pointed out that, based on the history of storm-cycles, there have been long weather cycles that could last for decades!

For about twenty five years, before 1995, there was a below normal hurricane cycle. After 1995, there was a gradual increase of hurricanes until 2004 when suddenly it hit a crescendo! The year 2005 might be a greater crescendo than 2004! This new cycle might remain until around 2020. Consequently, we can expect rough weather during the next fifteen years!

Given this cyclical scenario, it seems reasonable to expect at least five or six hurricanes to hit Florida every year.

The dire predictions by Professor Gray and by the National Weather Service were confirmed in late August 2005. <u>Hurricane Katrina</u> actually originated as a "tropical wave" from the west coast of Africa. Trade winds blew it westward and it became a "tropical depression number twelve" in the Caribbean islands. She seemed to disappear for a few days. Then, the warm Atlantic waters resuscitated her and she became a named storm in the Bahamas.

On August 26, Katrina became category 1 hurricane and battered North Miami! She crossed the state towards the Florida Keys. (The original prediction was that the hurricane would traverse the state towards Tampa and then make a second landfall at the Florida Panhandle.) Instead, the storm followed the natural law of least resistance and crossed the state where there was less land resistance.

While in the Gulf of Mexico, Katrina grew into a category 3 hurricane! On Sunday, August 28, <u>Katrina became a category 5</u>, with wind velocity of 175 mph! Katrina became a three-hundred mile wide monstrous, catastrophic storm and made a landfall on Monday, August 29, as a strong category 4 storm!

Katrina devastated New Orleans, Louisiana, Biloxi, Mississippi and Mobile, Alabama! Because of the magnitude of the storm, the damage extended into the Florida Panhandle and into the inlands of Louisiana, Mississippi, Alabama, Georgia, Tennessee and all the way to the northeast. Katrina caused wind damage and flooding in all those states.

However, <u>Katrina carried a storm surge of 29 feet,</u> the highest ever recorded in the country! A storm surge of 29 feet does not mean just one wave; in fact, it was a series of monstrous, obliterating waves that kept coming in every three or four minutes, while the hurricane was raging! Because the Gulf Coast regions, from east of New Orleans all the way to the Florida Panhandle, were very low and flat, the storm surges went in as a destructive *tsunami* and leveled all the buildings and killed thousands of people over a stretch of at least two miles deep and 100 miles wide! Storm surges were what killed people and animals and obliterated properties!

However, the city that suffered the worst damage was New Orleans! The city was built in a shape of a bowl and the lowest sections were twelve feet below sea level! To make the conditions even worse, the city was surrounded by the Mississippi River in the south and by Lake Pontchartrain in the north. The Lake was 41 miles long and 25 miles wide. The water in the Lake was actually higher than the city but an extensive levee system prevented it from flooding the city in the past.

However, when Katrina's storm surge hit New Orleans, <u>three sections of the levee were washed out</u>! One breach in the levee was over 300 feet wide. <u>Eighty percent of the city quickly</u> <u>went under</u> <u>water</u>, which was about twenty feet deep in some areas! Most of the buildings were flooded up to the eaves of the roofs!

It was estimated that at least 100,000 residents ignored the mandatory evacuation of the city! As the flood rose, residents climbed to the higher floors and into the attics! When the flooding reached the attic, some people broke through the roof and waited on the roofs for rescue! Others drowned in the attic because they couldn't break through the roofs!

New Orleans suddenly became a tragedy of biblical proportions because the sudden flooding was not foreseen even by the elected leaders! Thousands of evacuees went to storm shelters, like the Superdome, the Convention Center and eight other shelters, thinking that they would go home as soon as Katrina had passed through!

They wrongly assumed that their inconvenience was just a matter of few hours. They didn't bring with them any food or water! For five days, those evacuees, stranded in the storm shelters, didn't have any food or water! There were no toilets that functioned! The stench of feces, urine and unwashed bodies made life completely miserable!

Chaos immediately settled in and looters took advantage of the situation! The city police were overwhelmed because one third of them had disserted their stations! Gang members even shot at those who were trying to help!

Serious help from the military didn't arrive to the evacuees and the flood victims until eight days later! As could be expected, under such dire circumstances, many evacuees died or drowned! Some people who were stranded on their roofs were eventually rescued by helicopters but only after suffering from days of hunger and dehydration!

Every day, the author watched the sad scenes being shown by CNN! The images were those of exhausted, disoriented and starving families and crying children stepping around corpses, while they begged for water and food! They all seemed helpless and powerless; at the mercy of forces beyond their control!

What went wrong? It seemed everything! Leaders failed to lead! They hesitated; they froze because they were unprepared and overwhelmed by the actual reality!

However, the biggest agency that was obviously negligent was the Federal Emergency Management Administration (FEMA)! Michael Brown, the director of FEMA, who had been appointed by President Bush, didn't even know that there were over 25,000 evacuees in the Convention Center who needed immediate help!

President Bush himself was not above reproach! For years, the Army Corps of Engineers had asked for more money to bolster the aging earthen levees of New Orleans! The Bush administration, strapped by the war in Iraq and eager to hold down spending, actually reduced funding for the New Orleans levees! Bush should also be blamed for appointing Brown who was simply not qualified for the job! It was a political appointment!

Months later, Michael Brown revealed that he had informed the President and Michael Chertoff, Secretary of Homeland Security, that the levees were seriously in danger. In spite of the warnings, those leaders failed to do anything!

The real victims were the poor blacks who made up 70% of the city population. Virtually all those who didn't evacuate to safer places were blacks who didn't own cars and couldn't use public transportations. The city could have used school buses to take the poor and the elderly people to the storm shelters.

When the storm shelters got flooded, the evacuees needed to be rescued and moved to other storm shelters! The school buses couldn't be used to relocate them because, by that time, they were all under water! The evacuees in the Superdome had to be flown 350 miles away to Houston, Texas, to stay in the Astrodome.

By Wednesday, September 7, all the evacuees had been rescued and the giant pumps were pumping the water from the city. It may take months to dry up the streets but the pumps were working 24/7. Meanwhile, the widest breach on the levee had been temporarily plugged!

Mr. Michael Brown who symbolized incompetence and ineptitude was replaced by Vice Adm. Thad W. Allen as Gulf Coast director of FEMA on September 9, 2005. Homeland Security Secretary, Michael Chertoff, sent Brown back to Washington to be "the director for potential disasters." This could be a euphemism for a dead end job. It was the administration's lame attempt to cool off the political furor generated by the government's faltering response to Hurricane Katrina!

Almost two weeks after the hurricane had devastated miles of the west Gulf Coast shorelines, the public still did not understand why the aid to the victims took so long to even start! On September 10, Brown resigned from his job!

Brown's resignation opened up a faulty structure that paralyzed FEMA. In the past year, FEMA was autonomous and powerful. In 2005, FEMA was defanged and was assigned as a subordinate structure under an umbrella called Homeland Security. Michael Brown was suddenly a subordinate of Michael Chertoff. Brown didn't lift a finger or raised his voice to help the needy because he had no authority. He became the scapegoat for Chertoff, the secretary of

Homeland Security and the scapegoat for President Bush who acted as if helping the refugees wasn't his obligation!

****

New Orleans was a disaster waiting to happen for a long time! Built in 1718 by French settlers, the city was floating on decaying vegetation. For centuries, the city was sinking because it was built on semi-liquid foundation. As the foundation solidified, the city sunk further down.

The city was also sinking in many more senses of the word: the middle class and the educated young people couldn't find jobs in the city. Between 2000 and 2004, 30,000 residents moved to Atlanta, Dallas, Tampa and other cities. Between 1995 and 2000, metro Atlanta had increased by 91 persons from New Orleans per 1000 new comers; Dallas had increased by 60; while Tampa, Florida had increased by 146.

As white residents moved out, New Orleans became much more racially segregated! There were only two classes of people who remained in the city: those who were emotionally and economically entrenched in the city and those who had no where else to go. The latter were mostly poor blacks with little or no job skills. They lived in the eastern sections of the city, which should not have been populated. The land should be reclaimed by the swamp!

In order to survive, the business sectors of the community emphasized tourism as a last resort! This is the aspect of the city that many tourists will remember and understand.

There are a couple of positive notes about New Orleans. The French Quarters, which is where the city started, was spared from flooding because the historic district has the highest elevation! The other area that was not flooded was the Garden District, where affluent white residents lived. Because these two areas are at the core of the city, New Orleans will rise again from its ashes and the floods! The new city will be different and better: more vigorous and a place not just to visit but a place to live!

There was also good news about the flood in New Orleans. As of September 10, 2005, there were 35 large pumps working in the city to dredge the streets. The Army Corps of Engineers have also installed 40 temporary pumps to facilitate the drying up of the city. The original estimate of removing the flood waters was three months. As of September 10, two and a half feet of water have already been returned to Lake Pontchartrain. The new estimate of how long it would take to make the City dry has been cut down to only forty days. This is good news to the residents of the "Big Easy!"

****

Unfortunately, Hurricane Rita hit the Louisiana and Texas coasts only a week later. Rita undermined the levees again! Parts of New Orleans were flooded again but not as badly as with Katrina!

****

The tragedy in New Orleans and the other Gulf Coast states have shifted attention from Florida! The fact was that Katrina had first destroyed south Florida before she wrought havoc on New Orleans and the other Gulf Coast regions! The category 1 hurricane, when it devastated North Miami, actually killed eleven people in Florida.

The fact remains that, since the year1851, the hardest hit state has been Florida, with 110 hurricanes! The other vulnerable states are Texas, with 59 hits, Louisiana with 49, Mississippi with 15, Alabama with 22, Georgia with 20, South Carolina with 31, North Carolina with 46, Virginia with 12, Maryland with 2, Delaware with 2, New Jersey with 2, Pennsylvania with 1, New York with 12, Connecticut with 10, Rhode Island with 9, Massachusetts with 10, New Hampshire with 2 and Maine with 6. Indeed, Florida is the most vulnerable state!

With this disturbing profile of Florida, one might suspect that there has been an exodus of people from the state! Yes, there was an exodus, which started with the scourge of Charley! But those who left were the cowards and those with marginal financial means! Some residents of trailer parks and mobile homes have been forced to abandon their residences because the "terra firma" under their homes has been sold to developers who planned to build luxurious condos on the properties! The displaced Floridians were forced to move and live with relatives somewhere else.

In spite of the hurricanes and tornadoes, daredevils have still been coming to Florida because those people find storms, tornadoes, thunder and lightning exciting! In the past year, for example, people have camped out in the night for a chance to buy two-bedroom condos for $250,000! Some have even camped out to buy $2.7 million condos in Cape Coral!

It is interesting to note that one reason why life in New Orleans was deemed exciting was because it was besieged by dangers! Because the city, for the most part, was under sea level, flooding was a constant threat! The city had also been hit by many hurricanes! Residents of the city tended to have a *party spirit* because life in the "Big Easy" was shorter than normal!

Similarly, life in California has also been exciting because of the constant danger that the state may slide into the Pacific Ocean due to wide *fault lines and severe earthquakes*! When people's lives are threatened, individuals tend to live their lives more fully! Californians don't want to live anywhere else. The *constant sense of danger* is part of the culture and the ambiance of the state! The constant expectation of earthquakes naturally creates excitement!

However, if the truth is known, these *daredevils in Florida are not as brave as they might appear*! Many of them have second homes somewhere in the Appalachian Mountains or further north! They might experience the same storms up north but not as hurricanes. By the time the storms reach them, they will have been down-graded to mere tropical depressions! The storms become mere inconveniences but not deadly. As always, those who have *greater means have greater options*! "Asi es la vida." (Such is life.)

In spite of the four deadly hurricanes that ravaged Florida during the summer of 2004 and the deadly hurricanes Katrina, Rita and Wilma in 2005, the author adheres to his expectations that southwest Florida will remain as the safest area of the state! He expects the summer storms to follow their normal paths to the Gulf of Mexico and their landfall will be on the west side of the Gulf of Mexico or the Florida Panhandle.

Despite these scary predictions, the National Weather service researchers are gaining valuable insights in further understanding and predicting more accurately the pathways and the landfalls of the hurricanes! Greater accuracy of prediction will save millions of dollars in emergency preparedness and it will save a lot more lives!

Hurricane Charley was a good example of how far the weather service needs to improve in the accuracy of its predictions and weather analysis. Because the first landfall prediction of Charley was Tampa/St. Petersburg, the residents of Punta Gorda and Port Charlotte were largely complacent that they were out of harm's way! When Charley suddenly slammed into their communities, they were caught completely unprepared! That was an egregious mistake in hurricane prediction!

Because of the inaccuracy of weather predictions, the residents of Florida should take the hurricane predictions "with a grain of salt!" They should formulate at least two other emergency plans of action, in case the weather forecasters made a mistake. What happened in Port Charlotte and Punta Gorda in the summer of 2004 should never happen again!

Chapter Twenty Two.
Boom Market

When Yeta and Pol reinvested in real estate in 1988, they thought they would keep the properties for only five to ten years, on the assumption that the properties would appreciate in value quickly! How naïve and ignorant! For at least twelve years, appreciation had been virtually flat! They had to sell some properties to meet some extra expenses, like water and sewer assessments. The assessments came to about $12,000 per house.

In the last four years, however, southwest Florida has been experiencing a boom market! Since Cape Coral is geographically second only to Jacksonville in acreage, the boom is not uniformly felt! Since waterfront dictates prime value, the boom is occurring in waterfront neighborhoods, with a new architectural twists. The present architectural craze is Mediterranean, with Roman arches and columns!

The boom has been spreading like wild fire! Recently, the developer of Tarpon Point Marina, in southwest Cape Coral, announced the sale of seventy condos, which would constitute the third tower of a three-tower development! The first two towers had already sold out in a normal pace.

To the surprise even of the developers, potential buyers were camping out at night for a chance to buy a unit early the next morning! Ray Broderick, a real estate broker, didn't bother to camp out. He was quite sure that there was ample opportunity to buy seven condos for seven clients.

At eight o'clock the next morning, he carried with him seven fat checks representing seven affluent clients! Each check was for $25,000 to be used as security deposit. By ten o'clock in the morning, Broderick went home dejected and empty handed! All the seventy condos that ranged in price from $700,000 to $2.7 million had already been sold out in less than two hours! As it turned out, the former customers of the developer had the first crack on the available units! This meant that some of the buyers were investors, not users, and were looking to make a big profit later on.

Twenty-one real estate brokers put their names on a waiting list, just in case some buyers changed their minds.

The Tarpon Point Marina was a desirable development because they were a Naples, Florida, style of development and were high-end offerings! The complex would feature roof gardens, hot tubs, outdoor kitchens, a resort style swimming pool, waterfront shops and first class restaurants! The three towers development was called *Tarpon Landings*, which would be a gated community. There would be a total of 210 condo units in three fourteen-story buildings. All the three towers were still in blue print stages. The first tower would be finished in December 2005; the second tower in the summer of 2006; and, the third tower would be finished in sixteen months. This pace of sale had never been heard of before in Cape Coral!

However, there was a kind of precursor just a year earlier. In the same general area of development, home sites were going to be sold the next day. It was predicted that the homes sites would sell for at least a million a piece! Potential buyers, or persons representing them, were camping out overnight to buy the next morning! The reason why those home sites were deemed desirable was because they were the closest to the Gulf of Mexico! Among the bidders were residents of Port Royal, the expensive canal-front enclave of Naples, Florida. The bidders were trying to improve their Southwest Florida addresses---"closest to the Gulf of Mexico." Generally, the buyers were avid sailors and very rich!

Today, Cape Coral is among the hottest markets in real estate in the whole country! One of the hot selling enclaves is Coral Cove. Richard Halpern of The Prince Group said, "With today's spiraling costs, a condominium like this one could never be replicated again. It's an exceptional value, the likes of which we may never see again." Coral Cove is contiguous to Echo Park, a four mile nature preserve, equipped with meandering board walks that lead the walker to two fishing piers and a breath-taking view of the Midpoint Bridge and the skyline of Ft. Myers. The development is close to shopping centers, schools and hospitals. The Regional and International Airports are only twenty minutes away.

Last April 28, 2006, Cape Coral-Ft. Myers business communities were ranked by Inc magazine as number 3 in the nation among the hottest cities in business growth. Naples-Marco Island came in eight. Yuma, Arizona topped the list. Inc magazine is the leading magazine for entrepreneurs. The high ranking of Cape Coral-Ft. Myers is based primarily on job growth.

In ranking Lee County, where Cape Coral and Ft. Myers are situated, the magazine wrote, "Hurricanes haven't dampened the population growth in this Gulf Coast area---it is up 16 percent to more than 500,000, since 2000. Among the key job generators: tourism, construction and new service firms, many founded by refugees from cooler climes."

****

Since Pol and Yeta live on a Riverfront community in Cape Coral, Mike Darda of Century 21 Sunbelt Realty, sends them a quarterly newsletter about the real estate activities on the River. Mike specializes in high-end properties on the River or large canals. During the first quarter of 2005, some houses on the River were selling for three million or more. The average price for the period was $1,616,100. The average price has been rising throughout the year 2005.

Low-rise condos at Coral Cove   High-rise
condos at Tarpon Point

Even new developments, off water, were selling briskly in Cape Coral! Two new developments on Del Prado Extension, Entrada and Coral Lakes, had customers camping out overnight to buy two bedroom condos, which cost, on average, around $250,000.

An innovative style of housing called Coach Homes was recently started by Concordia of Cape Coral. Based on the preferences of three completely different focus groups, coach homes have the amenities of luxurious homes like tile roofs, arches, cathedral ceilings, granite counter tops and swimming pools but with limited square footage. Still, they average only about $200,000 for a two bedroom condo.

Concordia of Cape Coral is located in what is called the <u>New Cape Coral</u> because it is located in Kismet and Del Prado where the <u>Academic Community</u> will be developed. Part of the developments are university extension campuses and a <u>Major Environmental Park</u> designed to be the largest park in Cape Coral, a regional library and a <u>Festival Park</u> where all community festivals would be held!

For the first time, over a long period, condos are more popular among the new buyers! It seems that the new retirees want more leisure time and don't want to mow lawns or maintain gardens.

****

It was puzzling why real estate values were stagnant for so long; but suddenly there was such a demand! The author suspects that the demand is throughout Florida and probably throughout the whole country!

The state of Florida has thousands of miles of beaches and so many lakes. Then, there is the Gulf of Mexico and the Atlantic Ocean. Even the interior of the state has all sizes of lakes. Every year, new lakes are formed by a natural process called <u>sinkholes</u>. Sinkholes may also be natural catastrophes because they have swallowed up houses, cars, pets and trees. But, they are part of the natural phenomena in Florida. The reason why the state has sinkholes is because the underlying stones throughout the state are sandstones. This type of stone is soft and porous. This explains why there are also several miles of caves, streams and rivers underground.

<u>Lake Okeechobee,</u> in the middle of the state and west of Palm Beach, is so vast that one would mistake it for an inland Ocean.

****

The boom market arrived slowly about four years ago. During the last two years, it picked up steam! Last year, it became very hot because the "baby boomer generation" is preparing to retire and are positioning themselves and grabbing waterfront properties! There are 76 million of them.

There are only so many waterfront properties and so the demand has exceeded the supply! This sudden upsurge in the real estate market has given the Mabulbuls a chance to sell off five of their rental properties and further lessened their inventory and their responsibilities! The sales also lessened their fear of the Florida hurricanes and tornadoes because they have to worry only about their own home and five rental properties.

How long will this boom last? In the twenty-one years that Yeta and Pol have lived in Cape Coral, they have observed the pendulum swing from boom to bust and vice-versa only twice. Between 1988 and 1991, there was a short boom period! The boom turned to bust by 1991 because of an economic recession that plagued the whole country.

This time, however, the boom will last for a long time because the baby boomers are coming and there are so many of them! Between September 12, 2005 and December 2023, 88,500 baby boomers will turn 59&1-2 every week and become eligible to pull their money out of their retirement accounts, without penalty! Some of these boomers will also inherit millions from their affluent parents.

There is another important reason: home hunters have finally discovered that Cape Coral is a water wonderland and that the prices are still affordable, compared to the surrounding communities! The city has over 400 miles of navigable canals that lead to the Gulf of Mexico, to the Atlantic Ocean and to the rest of the world. Furthermore, the city is only about 30% built out. Hence, the city has a lot of room to grow. The roads in the Cape are not congested; Ft. Myers and Naples cannot make the same claims.

There is a more important economic reason, which holds true throughout the country. The mortgage rates have stayed low, even though the short term rate of interest has been rising. As long as the mortgage rates stay reasonably low, the buyers will keep coming.

Unfortunately, there is a nefarious element that might spoil a healthy boom! That bad element is the presence of greedy speculators who enter the real estate market just for the profit! There is a potential for highly inflated prices and the potential to form a big bubble that could burst very quickly! There is also a potential for the long term interest rates to go higher. The interest rate may reach a height that could dry up the housing demand!

Last July 12, 2005, the New York Times made a front page report of several real estate <u>hot markets that suddenly became cold</u>. Five years ago, for instance, the <u>Denver, Colorado</u>, market was experiencing double digit appreciation as Telecom employers like Qwest Communications International and Level 3 Communications added jobs and new home buyers to the market. The homes were appreciating at around 17 % per annum.

From December 2000 to September 2003, however, Denver lost about 74,000 jobs (about 6% of its job base). In spite of this actual downturn, most residents of the Denver area still had a rosy picture of the appreciation of their houses because they kept reading about the high appreciation of homes in other places such as Las Vegas, Nevada.

Tom Woods, a 37 year-old defense industry consultant was building a nest egg for one of his younger son's college education. Three years ago, he bought a three bedroom house in Parker, Colorado for $155,000. He expected his investment to grow at least $10,000 a year.

Last October 2004, he put the house up for sale to cover an unexpected medical expense. The house sat there empty for eight months without any takers. In order to finally sell it, he kept lowering the price. Moreover, he had to make all kinds of concessions, like paying the buyer's closing costs. After a three-year investment, all he netted was less than $10,000. He was very disappointed because he had expected to make a substantial amount of money!

Still, there are places like, Las Vegas, Riverside, Calif., Miami, Fl. and Washington where appreciation is still more than 20% a year.

By the end of the first quarter of 2005, the increase of value of Denver homes had gone down to 3 percent, according to the analysis by Economy.com, a research firm. The younger buyers have already made adjustments to the new reality. They were postponing making expensive renovations. They are now slow to move to a bigger house every two years. They are also learning that galloping price appreciation is not necessarily the norm!

Some real estate economists find this return to 3 or 4 percent appreciation as normal and profitable enough because it still beats inflation. The historic norm has been 4 to 6 percent appreciation.

There are analysts who take a gloomier point of view about what can happen to some places when the appreciation slows down to a virtual halt! "I think Denver is a best case scenario," said John Vogel, an adjunct professor of real estate at the Tuck School of Business at Dartmouth College. "In the case of Naples, Fl., Miami, Fl., Chicago and New York, I think you'll see dramatic price decreases because I think the prices have become artificially inflated by trading and speculation!"

Vogel was implying that the reason why Denver landed softly and safely on its feet was because it never really reached the heights of Las Vegas where prices increased by 33 percent just during the first quarter of 2005. Denver could have suffered a greater shock!

Denver, therefore, is a good cautionary tale because it is not out of the woods yet. The inventory of available homes in Denver has climbed from 8,010 in January 2000 to 25,817 in June 2005. It was taking much longer and harder to sell houses in the city. The sellers were using all kinds of incentives to sell, such as discounted mortgages, interest only mortgages and other creative ways of selling. At Sapphire Point, in Castle Rock, a builder was offering a $40,000 price discount. Another builder was offering an air conditioning. The competition will become even harsher and harder!

Even though real estate value is now going down in some sections of the Denver suburbs, it doesn't mean that the appreciation will die out completely. The primary engine of real estate appreciation is demand that is higher than the supply. Ten years earlier, in Calabasas, a suburb of LA, prices of homes were depressed, down by 40%. Yet, in 2000, Debbie Daly and her husband paid $402,000 for a four-bedroom ranch house. In five years, their $100,000 down payment was worth a million bucks. Because of the swinging pendulum between boom and bust, they decided to sell the house last year for $910,000 and rented a house nearby.

They were playing it safely and were waiting for the doldrums to hit the real estate market again. Then, they could buy a new house for much less money.

Not many people would "market time" the sale of a house especially if they loved it. Renting could change the quality of their lives; and waiting for the down turn could take ages to materialize. For example, the boom in the "sunbelt states" like Arizona and Nevada has been going on with double digit appreciations. Bust is not in the horizon for a while. Las Vegas has been seeing dizzyingly unbelievable prices for decades now!

Thomas Kunz, for example, moved from California to New Jersey in 2004 to assume the job of CEO of Century 21. Instead of selling his California house, which had appreciated from $335,000 to more than a million, he rented it out because he is betting that real estate will continue to appreciate in that state.

Jon Birger, of Money Magazine, asked Kunz whether double-digit annual gains was unhealthy. He responded, "The economy is basically good. Jobs are still plentiful and wages are still going up. It is still a good time to buy a home to live in."

Birger asked further, "But, what about places like Las Vegas or Miami, where more and more buyers are investors? Doesn't that increase the risk of a sell-off, if prices stop going up?"

"Sure, there are investors who get into real estate to buy and flip. But the majority of people are still buying because they need a place to live."

"Vacation homes are especially hot with some areas appreciating 20% to 30% a year. Can this continue?"

"Appreciation is determined by demand. In desirable areas, I expect you'll see demand remain fairly high. You've baby boomers who are saying, 'Geez, I'd like to have a place on the beach or in the mountains.' At the same time, over the next 10 years or so, an estimated 7 trillion to 10 trillion will be coming into their hands from their parents---people who saved every damn dime they could, paid off their homes, paid off their cars and didn't spend extravagantly."

Kunz' view about real estate in the whole country was confirmed by the figures reported by USA Today on July 25, 2005. The paper reported that sales of existing homes set a record in July, with home prices shooting up, the fastest pace in nearly 25 years. The fast paced sales helped to push the median price of existing homes up to a record of $219,000 last June 2005. This was a gain of 14.7% from the median of last year. This jump in prices was the biggest since November 1980.

The June performance was not expected in the light of what the Federal Reserve Chairman, Alan Greenspan's remark that there were flash signals that some parts of the country could be in the grip of "speculative fervor." Such a statement could have raised concerns among home owners that the price increases could not be sustained. It could then result in prices sharply declining if the long term interest rates started to rise, which would weaken the demand.

That situation could spell trouble for homeowners who will find the value of their homes falling below the value of the mortgage that they had obtained to finance the purchase.

The June 2005 sales were strong in all regions of the country. Sales in the West rose 5.5%. In the Northeast, sales rose 3.4%. In the Midwest, it rose 1.9%. And in the South, it rose 1.1%. Even though these percentages were not large, still the performance exceeded expectations because many economists predicted a "flat sales" because of strong increases in the previous months.

David Lereah, the chief economist of the National Association of Realtors explained, "The boom in housing is being driven by mortgage rates, which, defying expectations, have remained near rock-bottom levels this year even as the Federal Reserve has continued to raise the short-term interest rates."

The sales of both existing and new homes have set new records in the past four years. Many analysts are predicting that both sales groups would climb to record heights in 2005.

With the national figures pointing up, it is predictable that the boom market in Cape Coral and the rest of the state of Florida will continue for a while.

However, the March 2006 report from the local Association of Realtors shows that the volume of sales has gone down as much as 30% in some places because of higher mortgage rates. Nevertheless, the prices of real estate have gone up 12% in Lee County, 17% in Collier County and 17% for the whole state of Florida.

****

For Yeta and Pol, the real estate conditions in Cape Coral are just ideal! If they should liquidate the five remaining rental houses, in the next three or four years, they will obtain top prices!

To maximize the sales and the profit, when the time is right, they have considered asking each tenant to vacate the house so they could renovate it and make it look like new. Then, they intend to add cosmetic and artistic refinements that would appeal to the artist in the buyers. And, they would redo the landscaping so that the houses have a good curb appeal. In order not to pay sales commissions, they could advertise the sales themselves and show the houses to prospective buyers. In a boom market, even a minimal exposure to the market is sufficient to move the property.

If the boom continues for the next five years, their assets should at least double during the period! On the other hand, if the prices should fall and the appreciation returns to normal (between 3 to 4 percent), they will still have a bonanza because the rental houses have already appreciated normally through the monthly payment of the mortgages, tax shelters through depreciation and a great demand for a relatively modest starter homes. Their houses would appeal to at least 25% of the population for personal use or for rental.

The other easy alternative is simply to hold on to the status quo and do nothing! The houses will naturally continue to appreciate on their own. After ten more years, the mortgages would be paid off completely. All the proceeds will then be pure profit: the accumulated assets generated by Yeta's and Pol's scheme to start a new career and make money with virtually no capital! That is success with a small "s"! Many other people have done greater successes in different fields. Still, for much less effort, they believe they are just as happy as anyone could possibly be! They tried leveraged real estate investing with hardly any capital and succeeded phenomenally!

Chapter Twenty Three.
On Cruise Control

As of January 2005, Yeta and Pol had lessened their rental inventory to only five houses but the combined value is still worth over a million dollars. Moreover, In May 2005, they refinanced their Florida house and it was appraised at 1.2 million dollars. Their summer home in Boone, North Carolina, is worth about $500,000. They have reached a comfortable cruising speed, which maybe called, "on cruise control."

This means that they have so fine-tuned every aspect of their business, their investments and their personal lives so that they virtually take care of themselves. The income from the five rental properties more than covers all their living expenses. This is because the income has risen to their maximum potentials and the expenses have become minimal. For example, the debt services of each existing mortgage have gone down considerably because the remaining indebtednesses are very low. The monthly payment of principal and interest is less than $225 per house. The monthly rental is, on average, $925. Hence, the monthly profit just from rental houses is at least $3,000 a month.

Moreover, their other investments (construction loans, certificates of deposit, and others) are earning at least 8% a year.

There is no more pressure to sell any property because they are sufficiently liquid. What this means is that they have immediate access to cash when necessary so that they don't have to sell any property or borrow money to pay any unforeseen bills. Their investments are now well diversified! In order to cover any unforeseen expenses, they have scheduled the maturity of Certificates of Deposit every six months.

For over twenty-six years, they built their small business so that they could afford a leisurely lifestyle. Maintaining two homes and paying two mortgages was, for a long time, financially stressful. They juggled their financial resources and liquidated properties when necessary. They had suffered serious financial reversals when the stock market plummeted to the ground in 1987. They feared that they might go out of business and end up in a "poor house!"

After eighteen years of clawing back from their financial loses, they have finally recouped what they had lost and have been moving forward financially. They are now in a financially stable position, which they could only dream about for many years! Now they can finally say, "We have more than enough!" They never dreamed of becoming rich; they just wanted to have enough money to pay their bills and to afford their retirement, however long they might live!

They have been virtually retired for twenty years now. They have no idea how long they will live. Pol will be seventy-four in June 2006 but he feels no more than fifty. His standard line, especially to new acquaintances has been, "I'm seventy-three, going on fifty." His health is excellent and his mind is active and sound. Writing five books during the last five years has preserved his mental agility. However long he lives on this planet, he believes he has enough resources to support his lifestyle.

Yeta is also in her seventies and is reasonably healthy. She was recently diagnosed with type 2 diabetes but she has her glucose levels under control. They are very careful with their diet and they exercise every day. Their weights have been under control.

They had suffered a financial catastrophe in 1987 when the stock market crashed. That catastrophe won't be repeated itself because they have no money in the securities market. They could suffer serious damage from a hurricane! Fortunately, they have enough insurance to be able to rebuild their house. Their maximum liability is only 5% of the value of their house. Conceivably, a Great Depression could happen within their life time. Even if such a calamity should happen, they will be able to survive! They live on the bank of the Caloosahatchee River, which is part of the estuary of the Gulf of Mexico. They can survive on what nature provides them: blue claws crabs, shrimps, oysters, mussels, scallops and all kinds of shellfish. There are all kinds of fish such as mullets, sheep's head, spadefish, red drum and even sharks.

However, there is one calamity that they cannot protect themselves from: their mortality. Death is part of life! When it happens, they'll be ready to go!

****

About twenty-five years ago, Mack Blank, a friend, asked Pol, "What is your percentage of return from your real estate investments?"

Without carefully computing the total return, he responded, off the cuff, "We get at least 200%"

"Two hundred percent?" Mack exclaimed in disbelief! "Aren't you exaggerating a bit?"

"I'm not exaggerating, Mack. I'm making a rough estimate!"

Of course, Mack didn't believe him. His favorite investments then were Certificates of Deposit, which paid less than ten percent.

If Pol had carefully computed his total return, starting with positive cash flow (also called "cash on cash"), equity build up through monthly payments of the mortgages, savings on taxes through the use of depreciation and market appreciation through prevailing demands, the total return would have exceeded 200%.

This rough conclusion was recently confirmed by Robert Allen in his book, "Nothing Down for the 2000s." Years ago, he wrote a best seller entitled, "Nothing Down." Mr. Allen was among those who have greatly influenced Yeta and Pol in their real estate decisions.

Allen computed every profit, including penalties for late rents. He came up with <u>274% as his total return</u>.

Pol's rough estimate of 200% was close enough! However you look at the total return, they are simply awesome! Remember that the computation was only for one year. Since they have been in the real estate business for over 26 years, their lifetime return, thus far, would be over 7000%.

This computation, however, is far from complete or accurate. In business, how much you actually make depends on how much capital you had actually <u>invested and risked.</u> Since Yeta's and Pol's scheme of investing was heavily leveraged, they invested very little money of their own because they had very little money to start with. Their seed capital was only about $70,000, which was the profit from the sale of 216 Delhi St. Yeta had owned the trinity house, free and clear of debts.

That $70,000 is now worth over three millions and, during this boom market, that amount may double in value in five years. Without bothering to compute exactly their total return, it is obvious that the return on their $70,000 investment, thus far, is at least a million percent! Now, that is mind boggling!

These are among the reasons why the author believes that real estate is the best leveraged investment!

Furthermore, when you consider that they embarked on this new venture, as middle-aged people, with little or no knowledge and skills in the field, what they had accomplished in a short period of time was phenomenal!

The end!

www.ingramcontent.com/pod-product-compliance
Lightning Source LLC
Chambersburg PA
CBHW031833170526
45157CB00001B/290